No one knows how to change lives better than Gayla Congdon. No one. She disrupted my life by inviting me to meet Jesus within the lives of the poor. In *Disrupted*, Gayla will not only teach you the practicalities of short-term missions (on which she is an unmatched expert); she will also teach you how to cultivate a heart that is vulnerable to the presence of God in others. This book belongs on the shelf of anyone who longs to live a passionate life.

—*MARK YACONELLI*, PROGRAM DIRECTOR,
CENTER FOR ENGAGED COMPASSION

Gayla Congdon is an inspirational hero of the faith. She is living proof of what God can do when Jesus' mission becomes your passion. The Urban Saints team is so grateful to her and Amor Ministries for the incredible life-changing opportunities they have opened up to youth groups across the UK. We join with her in praying that these short mission trips will be catalysts to inspire young people to embrace a lifetime of radically following Jesus.

—*MATT SUMMERFIELD*, CEO, URBAN SAINTS, UK

Gayla Congdon, one of the leading practitioners in the short-term missions movement, understands the essential role of discipling short-term missionaries for long-term impact. Her spiritual discernment and expertise make her the ideal person to guide participants in making the most of their short-term experience.

—*DAVID LIVERMORE*, AUTHOR, SERVING WITH EYES WIDE OPEN

For over thirty years Hope International University has participated with Amor Ministries and has relied on Gayla Congdon's
wisdom to assist our students in making short-term mission
work a learning experience. Her passion for cross-cultural
evangelism is contagious. This book is just what many need to
get the greatest return on their investment.

—*DR. JOHN DERRY, PRESIDENT, HOPE INTERNATIONAL UNIVERSITY*

I love Gayla's passion for mission, her pragmatic approach to
changing the world, and her enthusiastic faith. I am so pleased
she has put her insights into writing. This is an incredible resource for mission teams and world changers.

—*CAROLYN KITTO, CONSULTANT, DIRECTOR, SPIRITED GENEROSITY,
SIDNEY, AUSTRALIA*

Working with Gayla is an incredible blessing. With contagious
zeal and authentic care for her audience, Gayla draws from her
years of experience in ministry to show Christian leaders (from
ministries of every size and scope from across North America)
how to keep their spiritual passion alive.

—*MIKE BUWALDA, PRODUCER AND HOST, CHRISTIAN LEADERSHIP
ALLIANCE WEBINAR SERIES*

CULTIVATING A MISSION-FOCUSED LIFE

disrupted

Gayla Cooper Congdon

Standard®
PUBLISHING

Cincinnati, Ohio

Published by Standard Publishing, Cincinnati, Ohio
www.standardpub.com

Printed in: United States of America
Acquisitions editor: Dale Reeves
Cover design: Faceout Studio
Interior design: Ahaa! Design

ISBN 978-0-7847-3571-8

Library of Congress Cataloging-in-Publication Data

Congdon, Gayla Cooper, 1954-
  Disrupted : cultivating a mission-focused life / Gayla Cooper Congdon.
    pages cm
  Includes bibliographical references.
  ISBN 978-0-7847-3571-8
1. Christian life--Meditations. 2. Evangelistic work--Meditations. 3. Congdon, Gayla Cooper, 1954- 4. Missionaries--United States--Biography. I. Title.
  BV4501.3.C657 2013
  266--dc23

                              2012037020

18 17 16 15 14 13   1 2 3 4 5 6 7 8 9

DEDICATION

To my parents, the late Bud and Virginia Cooper,
who not only gave me my faith but also a deep
and abiding passion for the church.

Thanks to Wendy Johnson and Erin Illingworth for their commitment to this book and the honesty they brought to making it better.

The Amor team has been encouraging and patient as they shared this journey with me, and I'm grateful.

Thanks to the team at Standard Publishing who committed to this project and patiently saw it through.

My thanks to all the people who inspired the stories told in the book.

I'm so grateful to the Amor board of directors, our national advisory board, and Hope International University for our relationship over the past thirty-eight years and their unwavering belief in my gifts as a preacher—especially my dear friend Sherman Pemberton.

Cliff and Carole Stabler guide Scott's and my path and are a reminder that discipleship is something we do for the rest of our lives. Thank you.

I've been strengthened by the great love of my family on both sides: the Coopers and Congdons. This includes Dean and Amy Mathis, Luke and Joel, as well as Wendy Johnson; my brother Mitch and his family; and the three men I love most in the world—Scott, Jordan, and Zorro!

Oh yeah, and thanks to Marty Andry!

Daily inspiration has come from those whom I've had the privilege of working alongside for more than thirty years of ministry in the locations Amor has served. That includes the disrupters from Urban Saints: Matt, John, Phil, and Mark. And so very important are the men and women who pastor our churches—I'm grateful for your remarkable commitment to keeping families together.

CONTENTS

Weekly Devotions for Cultivating a Mission-Focused Life

The year was 1966. School was over, and my friends and I couldn't wait to get out our swimsuits and meet up at the public swimming pool in town. After changing into my funky one-piece in the locker room, I had begun to make my grand entrance to the pool area . . . only to be upstaged by a buzz that seemed to have everyone in a state of frenzy!

What I soon discovered was that for the very first time, our pool would no longer be segregated. I was eleven years old. I remember that people were holding on to each other, crying, and expressing that they were worried the water was going to change color! Even at that young age, I couldn't believe people would act like that.

On a winter day three years before the experience at our local pool, I peeked out the window of our front room and saw a car pull into the driveway. Two people that I recognized as our minister and the woman who taught my Sunday school class were coming to my house! I remember thinking, *Am I in trouble?*

But I was not in trouble. Don "Pappy" Hinkle and Mrs. Woods had arrived that day to meet with my parents because I had accepted Christ and it was now time for me to be baptized.

On February 10, 1963, as an eight-year-old little girl with my knees knocking and my lower lip quivering, I walked down the aisle of First Christian Church in Hobbs, New Mexico, to be baptized. I remember that day as if it were yesterday. And as young as I was at the time, I have always believed that I knew exactly what I was doing.

That was the day my life was *disrupted*.

When Christ comes into our lives, he disrupts our worldview. The day I was baptized and the day at the swimming pool are interconnected because when God disrupted my life as an eight-year-old, I began seeing the world through his eyes. That is why three years later on a hot summer day, I was one of only a handful of people who welcomed our new friends of a different race to join us for a dip in the pool.

Matt Summerfield is CEO of Urban Saints, a 106-year-old youth and children's ministry in the United Kingdom. Matt introduced me to this word *disrupt* and his concept of it. It came as a result of his staff asking him to move the midmorning prayer time to the start of their day in order not to be disrupted in the middle of their work projects. Matt thought about it and said no to their request because he felt this disruption was needed as a reminder that God was the one in control of their projects—not them.

Quite often, after we've had a hard day's work building a home with a Mexican family, I get the opportunity to share my disrupted story with students around a campfire. I speak of a night when I was nine years old at Guadalupe Christian Camp, in a setting very similar to the one the students are in right then. When Pappy Hinkle asked the crowd who wanted to commit their lives to Christian service, I jumped up in response and made my way to the foot of the cross that was illuminated by the evening fire.

I hope the students can envision the courage it took for me to stand before the other campers, with the majestic Guadalupe Mountains as a backdrop, and make a promise to be a missionary to the poor.

I have kept that promise, and forty-nine years later I am still living out the commitment I made on that warm, summer night at junior camp. And it wasn't something I put off until I had a college degree in hand that prepared me for the mission field. I came home from camp that summer with a belief that I could change my world—now!

Through this book, my desire is to give you some essential tools and resources on how to take Christ's disruption and cultivate a mission-focused life. I want you to be prepared to serve others on a short-term mission trip as well as in the community in which you live. This book will also take you through a weekly study of biblical truths illustrated by disrupted stories that I pray will reveal to you daily those around you who desperately need the witness of Christ.

> *Cultivating a mission-focused life means that the disruptions aren't over even after you have returned and started unpacking your suitcase.*

My hope is that a mission-focused life will become a part of the fiber of who you are so that, whether you are impacting those in faraway places or close to home, you are sharing in the cost of disrupted living.

Know that going on a short-term mission trip might take you to a distant place far from the comforts of your home, but cultivating a mission-focused life means that the disruptions aren't over even after you have returned and started unpacking your suitcase.

So be open, because when God disrupts your life, he will probably change you in ways you never expected!

get out your passport!

The first time I went on a short-term mission trip was during my senior year in college, and it caused a major disruption in my life. At that time I was not contemplating a future in cross-cultural ministry. A friend who had interned at an orphanage in Tijuana, Mexico, the previous summer had begged me to go with her and some other students. I admit that I caved in to the peer pressure as we all agreed to go *just this one time!* And—I'm not going to lie—I went kicking and screaming.

I got more on that trip than I bargained for. If someone had told me that I would someday be serving in Mexico, I would have thought the person was crazy. But that trip impacted me so much that it started the work I have been doing for more than thirty years.

There was no preparation for going to that orphanage. No one took me through an orientation to train me on how to serve cross-culturally. And when I moved to the Tijuana Christian Mission at the age of twenty-three as a recent graduate of Pacific Christian College, I went merely with one class on missions under my belt and with a willing heart.

My first year in Mexico, I was invited to dinner at the home of a family from our church in Tijuana. I can still remember the look on the face of my gracious hostess when I inquired in my broken Spanish whether the meat they were serving had been refrigerated. My insensitivity still brings a tear to my eye, and I continue to be humbled by the grace that was shown to me by my brothers and sisters in Mexico in those early years.

Before You Go—Developing a Missional Mind-set

If you're going on a short-term mission trip, I want to help you be better prepared than I was that first time. Developing a missional mind-set before you go allows you to maximize your short-term mission trip experience. So what is a missional mind-set?

The apostle Paul's mind-set is perhaps best characterized in these words:

> Though I am free and belong to no one, I have made myself a slave to everyone, to win as many as possible. To the Jews I became like a Jew, to win the Jews. To those under the law I became like one under the law (though I myself am not under the law), so as to win those under the law. To those not having the law I became like one not having the law (though I am not free from God's law but am under Christ's law), so as to win those not having the law. To the weak I became weak, to win the weak. I have become all things to all people so that by all possible means I might save some (1 Corinthians 9:19-22).

Paul embodied a missional mind-set by setting aside his own freedom, comfort, and expectations so that he could understand and reach out to others. What you take into each situation, whether at home or abroad, is an expectation of what *should be,* based on what you have already learned. It is only when you experience what *is* that you truly begin to understand. We often remind ourselves to enter with the mind-set of a learner, not a teacher.

Ultimately, a missional mind-set means that the impact of the short-term experience cannot be allowed to fade away once you come home. When you return home—having been disrupted by those things that are different—you will see your surroundings in a new light. The trip you have taken becomes part of who you are.

Are you ready to start packing?

What to Pack and Unpack

If I were sitting with a group leader during dinner at our camp and he or she asked for my number-one tip for a successful mission trip, I would tell that leader to have the team repeat this phrase over and over again on the drive to the work site: "We are going as learners, and they are the teachers."

Just having that maxim as part of your mind-set will set the tone for the entire trip. It will help you refrain when you are tempted to teach the women how to clean their houses, and it will help you better appreciate the way they built their homes that they designed to fit into their community. It will also allow God to teach you through their stories of life, family, culture, faith, and tradition.

For years Sherman Pemberton, former missionary to Zimbabwe, and I trained teams that have traveled all over the world. The basic principles are what we call Pemberton's Four Laws,[1] which we believe to be the key to maximizing your short-term experience:

1. It's not wrong; it's just different.

     When serving in South Africa we have to remember that

South Africans don't drive on the *wrong* side of the road. They just drive on a different side of the road than those of us who live in the United States.

2. It doesn't matter *why*; it just matters *that*.
The orphanage director in Mexico instructed us to move manure down the hill for composting. When she changed her mind and asked us move it to the open field on the left, we didn't question it—we just did it.

3. Never assume.
Please refrain from saying things like "They have no concept of time" just because more than once they didn't arrive at the hour that had been set. Likewise, my friends from other cultures have learned not to assume that Americans care more about being on time than we do about taking time for relationships.

4. Look for alternate interpretations and ask more questions.
My first roommate at the Tijuana Christian Mission was pregnant and unmarried. I interpreted her situation to be that she was living at the mission because she was not welcome to live at home. As I asked more questions in my limited Spanish, I learned that, yes, her parents no longer wanted her to live with them—but it was because she had become a Christian.

Write those principles on your mind and heart, and learn how to live them daily. You don't have to go thousands of miles away to come in contact with people who are different from you—even if they speak the same language or share your ethnicity. In some ways, every relationship is a cross-cultural relationship. Pemberton's Four Laws, along with a learner's mind-set, will help you have a richer, meaningful experience that will follow you home.

> *My friends from other cultures have learned not to assume that Americans care more about being on time than we do about taking time for relationships.*

And in terms of things *not* to pack, before you go on your trip, unpack any attitude of cultural superiority or a belief that those you are working alongside should be grateful. Instead, pack an abundance of humility and commit, as author David Livermore puts it, to *Serving with Eyes Wide Open*.

you've finally arrived!

My family and I went to Europe for the first time about ten years ago. And even though I had been a missionary and had dealt with different cultures for more than twenty years, I went on that trip with an arrogant attitude—I could adapt to new surroundings anywhere in the world.

My in-laws picked up my husband Scott, son Jordan, and me at Charles de Gaulle Airport, and we headed straight to Chateau de Chantilly. I remember thinking how well I was transitioning from being in the United States one day and France the next.

That afternoon we stopped at an open-air market to purchase bread and cheese for our evening meal. I felt so proud to be eating just like the locals! Then something took over, and all of a sudden I couldn't breathe. I became overwhelmed by how foreign everything felt. My panicky feelings seem to have been triggered by a smell in the market that I couldn't identify. And instantly all I wanted to do was get in our car and leave. In that short moment of time, I felt homesick and wished I could just go home!

You can imagine my embarrassment when I realized that the pungent scent was nothing more than the yeast they were using to bake the bread I would soon be eating! It was something I had smelled before in my own mother's kitchen.

What was I expecting? Unconsciously, I had anticipated what to expect based on prior experience, not on what was actually coming.

If you have already gone on a short-term trip, your greatest challenge on the next trip may be to avoid bringing expectations from your prior experience. If this is your first venture out on a short-term mission trip, your challenge is equally great in that you don't know exactly what to expect.

Being Missional While You Are There

So what does it mean to be missional now that you are finally at the destination of your short-term mission trip? As a learner you need to begin by allowing those who are hosting you to lead—not just on day one but for the duration of the trip. It is the ultimate diffusion of ego and power when you put yourself in the hands of those you have come to serve alongside.

Hopefully, you have come on this short-term trip with the heart of a servant. That should come with a reminder that it is not about you. When the local pastor or missionary asks you to do something, even if it doesn't make sense to you or you think you know a better way, you follow instructions with that servant's heart you came with.

Years ago we made the decision at Amor Ministries that groups couldn't personally pass out donated goods in the communities in which they were building houses. Because we work through local pastors, we thought it best for all donations to go to them, allowing them to decide how they would be disbursed.

Many of our trip leaders were upset that we were taking away the opportunity for their participants to feel good about personally giving out the food, clothing, and toys they had brought to these poor and needy people. But the participants' need for immediate gratification was making it all about themselves. What can make it worse is an even greater, though maybe subconscious, need to have those we're serving alongside feel indebted to us.

Just recently one of our team members from Mexico, Fernando, began serving as a field specialist. He is now leading groups in house-building projects. Not too long ago he asked, "Why do the short-term mission trip groups come right in and begin assessing the needs of the Mexican families?"

> *The participants' need for immediate gratification was making it all about themselves.*

Fernando observed that some of our groups have a propensity to come in and immediately want to change things—which can be culturally insensitive at best and may rob people of their dignity at the very worst. For example, many families in Mexico have built an outhouse that most Americans would consider unsafe or unsanitary. It would be insulting for us to express critical judgment when this may be the very best that a family can afford; and it would be insulting for us to refuse to use the outhouse, because it would rob that family of their dignity. Similarly, we tell groups to never just assume that something on the work site is trash. What seems like garbage to us may be treasure to the family.

Being missional while you are on the short-term trip is the

acknowledgment that you are not *the* solution, but you can be a part of it. Ultimately, God is the answer. He was there before you came, and he will be there after you leave. God is present in even the world's most remote areas; and in most places you visit, God's work will continue through the local pastor and the church.

It means trusting that those at your short-term location know what they are doing. This will require a commitment on your part not to circumvent what the local pastor or missionary has put in place. You are there to support what they do all year long.

It means that even though you are tempted to furnish the family's home or buy a new toy for the sweet child at the orphanage, you don't do it.

> *You will go on this short-term trip to change the lives of those you are serving, and yet it will be your life that will probably be changed the most.*

As strange as it sounds, being missional while you are on the field is harder than being missional before or after the trip. You go because you want to help out those in need. More than likely you are from a developed country and serving in a place that is underdeveloped. Your heart is pure and in pain because of the overwhelming needs of the people that you are exposed to.

That is you being disrupted. Trust me when I say that you will go on this short-term trip to change the lives of those you are serving, and yet it will be your life that will probably be changed the most. You may never know how great the impact is on those whom you served, but you will continue to see the impact on your life long after the experience.

Being missional while you are there *can* be simple. As you enter someone else's culture, it is for the purpose of developing a relationship where you learn from each other, both parties are transformed, and the kingdom of God grows. When we take participants on short-term mission trips to our locations in Mexico along the border, we like to say that we are "changing lives on both sides of the border."

Leaving When Your Heart Is Broken

After all these years it still gets to me. There is not a time when I leave the field that my heart doesn't break. A breaking heart is a natural part of the process. After all, we've been willing to put ourselves in a place of vulnerability in which God can dramatically change us. People whom you would least suspect to break down do break down when they later describe their short-term mission trip and those they had the privilege of serving alongside. They've been deeply affected.

Years ago a youth leader told me what happened when his youth group bus pulled into the church parking lot after serving in Mexico for a week. As the driver parked the bus in front of the sanctuary, all the students were standing up in order to get a glimpse of the shiny, brand-new car parked there—the one that had an oversized pink ribbon on its roof.

Everyone was oohing and aahing over the car when a girl on the bus realized that her parents were standing next to it with huge smiles on their faces. While on the mission trip, she had missed celebrating her sixteenth birthday—but it looked like her parents hadn't forgotten.

The girl asked to be let off the bus, and everyone assumed

that she was going to run into her parents' arms, thanking them for their generous birthday surprise.

She most certainly ran off the bus, but not into her parents' embrace. Let's just say she didn't quite make it to the church restroom before she began throwing up. She couldn't reconcile how her two worlds were now colliding. More than likely, she and all the other young people had been exposed to unbelievable poverty for the first time in their lives. To the young woman returning home from that place, this shiny, brand-new car didn't mean the same thing as it probably would have just a week earlier—prior to the trip.

Her life had been *disrupted*.

welcome home!

I had a recent conversation with a church pastor who told me that he had been on several trips with our ministry some years ago. He shared about a little girl he had connected with in the field community, and how hard it was to leave her when his heart was breaking. What he didn't expect to feel was an overwhelming anger toward God. There were more whys than his abundant faith could answer:

- Why did she have to do without when others had too much?
- Why doesn't the first world see poverty as something they can solve for the third world?
- Why did he feel so responsible for this girl without even really knowing her?

Our son, Jordan, has grown up serving in Mexico. During the time between his college graduation and graduate school, he spent a semester working at Amor Ministries. Since he had never been to Puerto Peñasco, we thought it would be a good experience for him to work there. When he came home, it took us a couple of days to notice that he was barely eating.

While debriefing on his experience, Jordan told us about two dads who had approached him during the house build, begging to work with the group in return for food for their respective families. Jordan had felt helpless when confronted by the need and humility that had driven those men to beg. The feelings grew into guilt because he had been born into having everything he needed. He struggled to understand why, and he just couldn't eat.

> *When he came home, it took us a couple of days to notice that he was barely eating.*

In our thirty-plus years of working in Mexico, Scott and I couldn't remember encountering a father asking for help in this way. Mothers and children had often begged—but never a father. We understood Jordan's frustration.

Unpacking When You Return

How do you unpack those feelings of possible anger toward God or guilt over having more than enough food to eat when others are going without? Debriefing your recent short-term trip is crucial. It should begin with two questions: "What is God teaching me through this experience?" and "How can I integrate it into the rest of my life?"

Sherman Pemberton starts our summer debriefing with our summer intern team by breaking down what reentry should entail. It ought to include these elements:

- A backwards look at what has happened to you emotionally, spiritually, physically, and socially. Now that you are home, take the time to do this as soon as possible.
- A present look at what you believe has changed and what you have become. First, ask yourself, "Have I changed?"

Then if you *have* changed, *how* have you changed? Can others see this change in you? Each year we get letters from parents telling us of the change that has taken place in the lives of their children who went on our trip. One girl from Walnut Creek, California, wrote us herself to say: "Not only do you change the lives of the people in Mexico; you change the lives of every single person involved in the process."

- A look into the future to determine where you will go from here and what you desire to be and do as a result of this experience.

Before you look into the future, you need to finish unpacking. You may have some feelings of isolation as a result of the changes that are taking place inside you. This could lead to an attitude that causes you to be quick to judge those at home who seem as if they don't care about the people you just left behind.

When you return and people ask you how the trip went, remember—they weren't there. So they can't begin to understand the intensity of what you have experienced. Tell them your favorite story of an event or person—and keep it short. Don't get your feelings hurt if that is all they want to hear.

Jordan had a choice to make when he returned from Puerto Peñasco. He could have told his dad and me that we should be doing more, or he could have isolated himself from friends and family who didn't understand why he was going without food. Instead, we discussed together our commitment to learning how to create sustainable food sources and teaching those in poverty how to do that for themselves.

One of the results of a short-term mission trip should be that your own personal "ecosystem" has been disrupted in a way that moves you to action. You will not view your material resources the same. Things that you thought you absolutely needed, you will now realize are only wants. You will now see people through God's eyes. This new perspective may confront your previous attitudes and stereotypes that need to be addressed. And you will be more cognizant of the suffering of others and, hopefully, have committed not to participate in their exploitation.

Living a Mission-Focused Life 365 Days a Year

One of the main questions that I get asked by people who have returned from a short-term mission trip is: "Now that I'm back at home, how can I make sure I don't forget what I've learned?"

How *do* you apply to your daily life what you've experienced? These people return all gung ho to do something significant because of the impact the trip has made on them. But often, within a few short weeks, they fall back into their normal routine as the trip begins to fade . . . and then becomes a distant memory.

Maybe you are a family who has just returned with a heart to serve together. Or maybe you're a student who has come home determined to make a difference in your community. Whatever the case, God wants you to return with a hunger and desire to continue changing your world!

In fact, don't wait until you return home; the moment to begin is on your *way* home.

I remember reading in *Stepping Out: A Guide to Short Term Missions* how God wants us to integrate our experience into every aspect of our disrupted lives. You may have been gone for a week, ten days, a summer, or a semester; after your return home you should translate what you left back on the field into how you live daily.[2] Additionally, I believe that by living out what you have learned, you will honor those people you just served.

Make a commitment now to take the next fifty-two weeks to listen to God. He wants to disrupt your life on a regular basis. If you want your short-term mission experience to be more than just a faded memory, then make it your life!

> But often, within a few short weeks, they fall back into their normal routine as the trip begins to fade . . . and then becomes a distant memory.

That's what Rob Taylor did. His first mission trip with Amor was in 2005. He refers to Amor mission trips as "his gateway drug." After four mission trips to Mexico and other countries, he has now moved his family of six to Swaziland to minister to orphans there. After reflecting on his short-term mission trips, he realized that he was called to serve God with his life—and that is what he is doing.

So what are you going to do now that you've returned home?

Weekly Devotions
for Cultivating
a Mission-Focused Life

i can't miss!

David said to the Philistine, 'You come against me with sword and spear and javelin, but I come against you in the name of the LORD Almighty, the God of the armies of Israel, whom you have defied. . . . All those gathered here will know that it is not by sword or spear that the LORD saves; for the battle is the LORD's, and he will give all of you into our hands'" (1 Samuel 17:45, 47).

Who did David, a young shepherd boy, think he was in committing to fight against the Philistine Goliath—a man who was over nine feet tall? Goliath had insulted the nation of Israel and put forth a challenge to any man in King Saul's army to fight him. David responded by saying he could do it, as he had already taken on lions and bears. He must have thought, *What's the big deal about an arrogant giant?*

David's oldest brother, Eliab, thought it was a joke. Already a member of King Saul's army, he wasn't offering to take on Goliath. Eliab even mocked David by telling him to mind his own business, which seemed to suggest that David return to tending his measly flock of sheep (1 Samuel 17:28). Can't you just hear the sarcasm dripping from Eliab's voice?

Was David confident in what he could do? No, but he was confident in the Lord Almighty and what *he* could do. David had grown up seeing God be victorious over and over again. So after he decided to fight the giant, using only a slingshot with five little stones, what do you think was going through his mind as Goliath came charging toward him?

My husband, Scott, uses this story of David and Goliath as an example to those who come on mission trips with us. He explains how overwhelming poverty can be—especially for those trying to build houses for the poor. Since 1980, Amor Ministries has built almost seventeen thousand homes in Mexico and around the world; yet the need is so great, the Mexican Housing Authority estimates that Mexico still has a deficit of nearly nine million homes.[3] Sometimes it feels like the problem is so big, what we do doesn't make a difference.

> *Was David confident in what he could do? No, but he was confident in the Lord Almighty and what he could do.*

David could have looked at Goliath and told himself, *He's so big and overwhelming, and no one—not even my brothers—believes I can kill this guy!* My husband looks at it differently, thinking it was probably pretty simple to David. He looked at Goliath and believed, *This giant is so big, I can't miss!* David's story proves that no matter how big the problem, whatever we do makes a difference.

Now that you have returned home from, hopefully, a life-changing mission trip, how will you continue making a difference in your daily life? Many opportunities are awaiting you in your own community. The question you should be asking yourself is, *Where can I begin serving now that I've returned home?*

Be like David. With the Lord Almighty on his side, he couldn't miss! Commit to being missional now and serve somewhere. One of my favorite slogans is taken from a World Vision poster that asks, "How do you feed a hungry child? One at a time." That's pretty profound and yet affirming that you can change your world by just doing something. Don't wait until the next mission trip comes around. Do something now. And like David, you won't miss!

Disruptive Questions

1. When have you felt like David as he faced Goliath? Has someone ever told you that you weren't capable of doing something, when you believed you could? What did you do?

2. Identify some specific "giants" in your community that need to be defeated. If you were to act like David, and pick up a sling and five little stones, which problem would you slay first? Why?

3. In what specific ways do you feel you are gifted to help others? Find a place to serve this week by using one of your gifts.

the great adventure, part I

In the book *Leading at the Edge*, we learn about two expeditions that took place about a year and a half apart in the early 1900s. The first one departed on August 3, 1913. This Canadian expedition, led by Vilhjalmur Stefansson, "set out to explore the frozen Arctic, between the northernmost shores of Canada and the North Pole."[4] The other expedition, the British Imperial Trans-Antarctic Expedition, was led by Sir Ernest Shackleton. It departed on December 5, 1914, from the island of South Georgia in the Southern Ocean. "Its goal was the first overland crossing of Antarctica."

Both ships, Stefansson's *Karluk* and Shackleton's *Endurance*, found themselves in eerily similar circumstances, though they were in different locations. Both groups faced a desperate fight for survival after their ships became trapped in ice. But the way the two leaders handled their ordeals, and the outcomes of the two adventures, were *not* similar. In fact, they "were as far apart as the poles each leader set out to explore."

As months dragged on, the crew of the *Karluk* did not

respond well. Team spirit disintegrated into self-interest, lying, stealing . . . The results were tragic: all eleven crew members died.

> *The way the two leaders handled their ordeals, and the outcomes of the two adventures, were* not *similar.*

The situation of the *Endurance*, however, played out in a totally different way—though the circumstances were every bit as desperate as those of the other ship's members. In spite of the extreme cold and a dwindling food supply, this group exhibited "teamwork, self-sacrifice, and astonishing good cheer. . . . It was as if the *Endurance* existed not just in a different polar region, but in a different, contrary, parallel universe."

This is how I see the great adventure of the twelve who were chosen by Jesus to be his followers. They were just ordinary people, and yet they were the ones whom God used to do something extraordinary. Many were imprisoned and martyred so that the good news of Jesus could be known throughout the world. And just like the men on the expedition, how they responded to Jesus' call made all the difference.

Regarding the early disciples, J. B. Phillips said,

It is heartening to remember that this faith took root and flourished amazingly in conditions that would have killed anything less vital in a matter of weeks. These early Christians were on fire with the conviction that they had become, through Christ, literally sons of God; they were pioneers of a new humanity, founders of a new Kingdom. They still speak to us across the centuries. Perhaps if we believed what they believed, we might achieve what they achieved.[5]

They were ordinary people—fishermen, tax collectors, and tentmakers—who did extraordinary things.

Cultivating a mission-focused life involves recognizing that God wants to use us to be a witness of his enduring love. My life is a testimony of how God uses ordinary people to accomplish extraordinary things. I am humbled daily by what he has done through this little girl who grew up in a small town on the West Texas/New Mexico border. All because I was willing to participate in his great adventure. How about you?

....
Disruptive Questions

1. Ordinary people accomplish extraordinary things all the time. If time, money, and resources were no object, what would be your great adventure for God?

2. What are you afraid of that is keeping you from this adventure? How can you resolve those fears and move forward in partnering with God?

3. Every ordinary person who's done something extraordinary made a sacrifice. What are you ready to sacrifice?

the great adventure, part II

What are some of the characteristics of ordinary people who do extraordinary things? I'm sure there are a lot more than I have time to enumerate here, but we'll go with these five for starters.

1. Those on great adventures recognize the role God plays. They trust that if he wants them to do something, he will give them the power and resources to do it.

Steve Horrex left Canada as a twenty-one-year-old, believing that God wanted him to serve in Mexico. Thirty years later he is a testimony to the fact that God gave him the power and resources to design the first home built by Amor Ministries in the Tijuana, Mexico, dump. Steve created the house designs that we still use, and today almost seventeen thousand families have shelter throughout the world.

2. Those on great adventures understand that they will face problems and obstacles. How they deal with them determines whether or not they accomplish the extraordinary.

3. Those on great adventures understand that at times

they will be afraid. Moses was afraid to lead the children of Israel. Peter became afraid in his attempt to walk on the water. Even Jesus asked God to "remove this cup" from him in the Garden of Gethsemane—referring to God's asking him to give his life on the cross (see Luke 22:42, *KJV*).

Moses ultimately led the children of Israel to the promised land, and that was extraordinary. Peter helped establish the church, and that was extraordinary. Jesus did give his life, and that was *beyond* extraordinary.

> *Those on great adventures understand that*
> *they will face problems and obstacles.*

4. Those on great adventures understand that at times they will fail. Failing is not the worst thing that can happen to someone. In his book *If You Want to Walk on Water, You've Got to Get Out of the Boat*, John Ortberg relates the story of Sir Edmund Hillary, who made several attempts at scaling Mount Everest before he finally succeeded.

After one attempt he stood at the base of the mountain and shook his fist at it. "I'll defeat you yet," Hillary said in defiance. "Because you're as big as you're going to get—but I'm still growing." Ortberg says, "Every time Hillary climbed, he failed. Every time he failed, he learned. Every time he learned, he grew and tried again. And one day he didn't fail."[6]

5. Those on great adventures know that they must continue to go forward. Teddy Roosevelt said,

It's not the critic who counts; not the man who points out how the strong man stumbles, or where the doer of deeds could have done better. The credit belongs to the man who is actually in the arena . . . who at best knows in the end the triumph of high achievement, and who at the worst, if he fails, at least fails while daring greatly, so that his place shall never be with those cold timid souls who neither know victory nor defeat.[7]

Thank God for people like the legendary missionary from Scotland, Dr. David Livingstone, who helped open the heart of missions to Africa because he was willing to go. And for Elisabeth Elliot, who was willing to return to Ecuador for two years as a missionary to the very tribe that had killed her husband, Jim.

In Ephesians 3:20, 21, the apostle Paul promises us that God gives the ordinary the courage to do the extraordinary: "Now to him who is able to do immeasurably more than all we ask or imagine, according to his power that is at work within us, to him be glory in the church and in Christ Jesus throughout all generations, for ever and ever! Amen."

Disruptive Questions

1. Do you have issues of trust as it relates to God taking you on a great adventure? If so, how can you get beyond these issues?

2. What specific resources do you need in order to move forward with God on your great adventure? Why do you think the fear of failure and the potential for embarrassment cause so many to not even take a chance on a great adventure?

3. Sir Edmund Hillary failed many times before he reached the extraordinary. How will you deal with failures along the way?

commit to a
great adventure

I n Genesis 37–50 we read the account of Joseph's life that took him from his father's home in Canaan to being sold into slavery by his brothers to becoming the second most powerful man in Egypt next to Pharaoh.

During this time Joseph was falsely accused by the wife of Potiphar, the man in Pharaoh's guard who had bought Joseph to be a servant. Joseph landed in prison, but eventually he developed favor with Pharaoh as an interpreter of dreams.

In those dreams Joseph saw the future of Egypt as seven years of abundance followed by seven years of famine. His plan was to store grain during the time of abundance in order to be prepared for the years of famine. During the famine people from other lands had to purchase their grain in Egypt because the Egyptians were the only ones who had prepared for the drought.

Among those who came to purchase grain were Joseph's own brothers. God used Joseph's betrayal by his brothers for the good of Egypt and beyond. At the end of Joseph's life, his great adventure came full circle; and eventually he was reconciled with his brothers and reunited with his father, Jacob.

The dramatic story culminated when Joseph spoke these kind words to his brothers, who feared his revenge: "Don't be afraid. Am I in the place of God? You intended to harm me, but God intended it for good to accomplish what is now being done, the saving of many lives. So then, don't be afraid. I will provide for you and your children" (Genesis 50:19-21).

Do you think if God had given Joseph a peek at what was ahead for him, he would have committed to go? Perhaps God doesn't do that for us because we probably wouldn't decide to go on the journey he has for us. Yet it is in these great adventures where we often learn to trust God for the outcome—no matter what it is.

Scott, Jordan, and I took a sabbatical in 2010 that was another great adventure for our family. On the recommendation of several people, we arranged to spend a week at Taizé, an ecumenical community in Burgundy, France. Taizé is described like this: "It is composed of about one hundred brothers, from Protestant and Catholic traditions. . . . The community has become one of the world's most important sites of Christian pilgrimage. Over 100,000 young people from around the world make pilgrimages to Taizé each year for prayer, Bible study, sharing, and communal work."[8]

> *Yet it is in these great adventures where we often learn to trust God for the outcome—no matter what it is.*

The first day we were there, all three of us wanted to leave. Jordan would later admit to me that he was asking himself,

What has my mother gotten us into this time? I remember thinking that I would endure the week just to prove to myself that I could.

The leaders were making us sit in silence for long periods of time, and we were singing the same songs over and over. And from our perspective, they were starving us. Additionally, it was extremely hot and humid, which just zapped the little energy we had from having so little to eat.

One of the leaders said on the first day that the times of silence would seem like they went on forever but by the end of the week we wouldn't want them to end. He was right. Over the next seven days, what seemed excruciating in the beginning became a real time of worship and introspection that none of us had ever experienced. We can't wait to go back.

The next time you are contemplating heading out on a great adventure, even though there may be some uncertainty in the back of your mind, you can tell yourself what my friend Amy Mathis says in situations like these: "Tough it out for Jesus." Then trust God for the outcome.

Life-Challenging

DISRUPTION

Every four weeks you will be given a challenge so that you can continue to live a mission-focused life. Your life challenge this month is to commit to reading the rest of this book so that you can allow your life to be disrupted.

Here are some practical suggestions for how to do that:

- Set aside a time each week to read the devotion and reflect on the questions given you. Block this time off in your calendar.

- Invite friends or family members to join you in reading this book so that you will have a partner to keep you accountable.

I encourage you to sign this challenge, every time, as a promise to the Lord that you will make the following sacrifice for his glory. Then follow through with your commitment.

Lord, this month I commit to reading the rest of this book, allowing you to disrupt my life.

Signature _____ Date _____

consider it pure joy

onsider it pure joy, my brothers and sisters, whenever you face trials of many kinds, because you know that the testing of your faith produces perseverance. Let perseverance finish its work so that you may be mature and complete, not lacking anything" (James 1:2-4).

That has been my go-to passage every time I'm in a situation where I am asked about my favorite Bible verse. If my memory is correct, I learned it when I was in Bible college, and it has just stuck. But there was a time when I wasn't sure if it was my favorite anymore.

A few years ago, with thirty years of ministry at Amor Ministries looming on the horizon, I was living *la vida perfecta* (the perfect life). The ministry was taking more than twenty thousand people a year on short-term trips, we had a large staff that covered all our bases, and we could afford to purchase any resource we needed to do ministry. Never in my wildest imagination would I have believed that the ministry would be presented with "trials of many kinds."

In 2009, it became increasingly evident that people were afraid to come to Mexico on short-term mission trips, as a result of the drug cartels. It was a huge disappointment to see cancellations that would eventually drop our numbers in half. More importantly, it broke our hearts to tell families that the building of their houses would have to wait.

We believed we had survived that difficulty, when a new plague hit: the swine flu. In the month of May that year, over half of our summer groups canceled as this last piece of news became the final straw for them.

We were experiencing the perfect storm. I was beginning to wonder whether, when I turned on the faucets in our office restrooms, blood like that from the plagues in Exodus would come out!

While our faith was being tested, we were committed to keeping our staff intact. We raised money, took pay cuts, had a garage sale, and rented out one half of our office space. Yet losing half of our yearly participants was just too much for the ministry to handle.

> *I was beginning to wonder whether, when I turned on the faucets in our office restrooms, blood like that from the plagues in Exodus would come out!*

In all our years of ministry, we had never laid anyone off; and there was not one person who warranted that outcome. Our board told us in August of that year that we had no choice—we would have to make cuts, and that would include letting some of the staff go.

It was not easy. There were many tears and heartaches.

Some tough decisions were made by the leadership of the ministry. Amazing people who had served the ministry well had to be laid off. And that hurt.

My husband and I are not the kind of people who let a trial like this keep us from moving forward. Our experiences over the years reminded us that this wasn't the first time we had to persevere—and it wouldn't be the last.

God knew exactly what he was doing with Amor Ministries during these challenging times to make it healthier and stronger for another thirty years. He allowed these disruptions so that we might be "mature and complete, not lacking anything."

Scott and I believe that our best years of ministry are ahead of us and that this season in the life of the ministry was preparing us for the future. Yep, we consider it pure joy.

When you encounter obstacles—which you will and may already have—I encourage you to see them as opportunities to become more like Jesus. During these times, you will witness God's promise to never leave or forsake us (Hebrews 13:5).

··
Disruptive Questions

1. When have you gone through a time of struggle that felt like a plague at the time?

2. In what ways did your trial by fire make you more mature and complete?

3. What do you hope will be your joy in the next season of your life?

a house built on the rock

G rowing up in the church, one of my earliest memories in Sunday school was learning the song "The Wise Man Built His House Upon the Rock," which is based on Matthew 7:24-27. The hand motions that went with the song made it even cooler, in my mind. The words tell the story of two builders—one wise and one foolish. The wise man built his house upon the rock (as the title points out), and when the rain and winds came, his house stood firm on that rock.

The song went on to tell that the foolish man built his house upon the sand, the floods came up and the rains came down, and the house on the sand went splat! (I loved that part because I could slap my hands together and make the *splat* sound!) The song's big finish was a call to build your house on the Lord Jesus Christ in order for it to stand firm.

Jesus told this story of the wise and foolish builders at the end of his Sermon on the Mount. The Sermon on the Mount, from Matthew 5–7, contains moral lessons for us to live by, as well as some of Christ's most well-known teachings, such as the Beatitudes and the Lord's Prayer.

These teachings are meant to compel us to take action.

We can't just go around *saying* we are Christians—our actions should show it. The impact of the Sermon on the Mount is why we are as committed to building houses with those in need as much now as we were in the early years at the Tijuana dump. Well, that and the story I'm about to tell you.

Tijuana was experiencing an El Niño weather pattern, and the city was devastated by the torrential rains. People were losing their lives, and hundreds of homes were being swept away in the floods. But Amor kept on building.

We can't just go around saying *we are Christians—our actions should show it.*

One of the houses being built was for a single mom and her five-year-old son. They had literally been living under a tarp, with very little covering to keep them warm. My husband, Scott, remembers the mom and her little boy smiling as they saw their house going up each day.

At the end of the build, the mother came to Scott and pulled out a picture of a baby. In Spanish she told him that she wanted him to have the picture. He inquired whether the picture was of her little boy. Shaking her head, she said no—it was her baby girl.

Scott asked the mom if he could see the baby girl, only to be told that she had died of pneumonia during the cold, winter rain.

Then the mother said these words to him: "My little boy and I now have a warm place to live. My baby girl is gone, and that cannot be changed. I'm giving you the only picture I have of her to remind you to never—and I mean never—quit building homes."

That week a house was built upon the rock. After more than thirty years, we still don't just *say* we are Christians.

Disruptive Questions

1. During bad weather how can you get beyond yourself to see how others are really suffering?

2. Have you ever experienced a stormy season in which you kept building on something (either literally or figuratively) and your perseverance paid off? What happened?

3. What is it that transforms you from being a Christian in name only to being one who also shows it with your actions?

it still gets to me

I have always been a person who feels deeply about the suffering of others. My family was attending a Little League game when I was about eleven years old, and I noticed that a group of kids were picking on a boy who was disabled. It made me so mad that I took it upon myself to push the bullies off the bench where they were sitting.

My memory tells me that there were about four of them to the one of me. I think you can imagine the horror of those boys' parents when they realized that a girl had been the one who had taken on their sons! And can't you just visualize me sticking out my tongue at them as their parents led them away, embarrassed by what had just happened?

When I graduated from Pacific Christian College in 1977, I went to live at an orphanage in Tijuana, Mexico. That experience was life altering in so many ways. It was there that I began to develop some of my views of ministry. I determined that I never wanted to get to a place in serving others where their pain and suffering no longer got to me.

In my interactions with some of the missionaries with whom I came in contact, I could see that some jadedness had crept in; they sometimes saw what they were doing as more of a job than a ministry. That seemed to have replaced the compassion that I believed had once been there. I remember telling myself when I was twenty-three years old that if I ever got to a place where my heart no longer broke over what broke God's heart, I needed to do something else.

But I can honestly say that after doing what we do for thirty-two years, it still gets to me. Several years back we were having a group photo op at the site of our ten-thousandth home. The house had been built for two sisters who were seventy-five and eighty-five years old—and they worked right alongside us! They had been living in a shack with no floor or windows or door. I tried to imagine my parents living like that, and it broke my heart.

One of the sisters took my hand and told me that this was the first real home she had ever had in her life. We both began to cry, and I reminded myself how much I despise poverty and that encountering it still gets to me after all these years.

What do you think *got to* Jesus? In Matthew 21:12, 13, I think we get a glimpse of what got to him. "Jesus entered the temple courts and drove out all who were buying and selling there. He overturned the tables of the money changers and the benches of those selling doves. 'It is written,' he said to them, 'My house will be called a house of prayer,' but you are making it 'a den of robbers.'"

Jesus was angry because people were being exploited. For a fee, money changers at the temple were exchanging a person's foreign currency into coins that were acceptable in the temple. Those in charge of selling the doves that were needed for a sacrifice were selling them for a profit. They were exploiting the concept of supply and demand. And this got to Jesus.

> *I remember telling myself when I was twenty-three years old that if I ever got to a place where my heart no longer broke over what broke God's heart, I needed to do something else.*

My office at Amor looks out over the Tijuana, Mexico, hills. Every day I have a visual image of what needs to be done. I cannot change things for everyone, but with God's leading and the help of others, we can change things for many.

And after all these years, it still gets to me.

Disruptive Questions

1. What things get to you? Why?

2. Read Matthew 21:12, 13 again, perhaps in another Bible version. What does this passage say about how the business of the church should look different from the business of the world?

3. Does it ever get to you when people are exploited? Have you ever asked, "Should we act to stop this?" When? What are some of the things that have gotten to you, and what are some practical steps you can take to alleviate the problems?

it just might hurt

n my junior year of high school, our class was informed that when we returned in the fall for our senior year, everyone would be required to get a tuberculosis shot. For some reason I obsessed about it all summer, fearing that it just might hurt. But in the end, the prick of that shot hurt much more in my mind than in reality.

When I think of physical and emotional pain in the Bible, I mentally take a walk in the Garden of Gethsemane. Here we have a picture of Jesus before his crucifixion: "And being in anguish, he prayed more earnestly, and his sweat was like drops of blood falling to the ground" (Luke 22:44).

Luke is "the only Gospel writer to mention the bloody sweat, possibly because of his interest as a physician in this rare physiological phenomenon, which spoke eloquently of the intense spiritual agony Jesus was suffering."[9] In the Garden of Gethsemane, Jesus was experiencing intense emotional pain while facing what many believe to be the worst form of capital punishment that has ever been. This all happened because of the cost of entering into a relationship with us. Jesus entered into our broken world.

If we are going to take on the nature and character of Christ, then part of our cost of cultivating a mission-focused life is to enter into others' brokenness. The Fuller Youth Institute, noting the focus of the book *Deep Justice in a Broken World*, says,

> It probably doesn't take a long list of statistics to convince you that our world is broken. Mission trips, service projects, and supporting children through relief organizations are just a few of the ways that many youth workers engage their students in serving the least, the last, and the lost. As good and helpful as these things may be on the surface, that's where they remain—at the surface. The problems run far deeper than an occasional paint job or fundraising project can solve. But it's not hopeless.[10]

But in order to address these issues of deep justice, we must enter into relationship with those who are broken. Just like Jesus did with each of us.

We will never experience the physical pain that Jesus did when he went to the cross. Most of us will never be asked to put our lives on the line and die as a result of serving on the mission field. But in order to address these issues of deep justice, we must enter into relationship with those who are broken. Just like Jesus did with each of us.

Several years ago while working at a youth camp, I shared some of the experiences I have had over the years while serving all over the world. As I was telling a story about a family receiving the keys to their home in Mexico, one of the women asked me to stop. She simply said, "I can't let myself go there. It's just too painful to hear."

I understand why she felt that way. I told her that just because I can talk about it so freely doesn't mean that the pain of seeing people suffer has gotten any easier for me. I must attempt to understand their pain in order to be compassionate when I serve them.

I can't relate to what Jesus experienced when he died on the cross. But I can allow my life to be disrupted each day as I intentionally put myself in places where brokenness exists. And each day I can choose to live in a way that tries to change that—even if it just might hurt.

Life-Challenging
DISRUPTION

Your life challenge this month is to read the account of Jesus in the Garden of Gethsemane in the Gospel of Luke (22:39-53). Then commit to volunteer for something that breaks your heart like it breaks Jesus' heart.

Here are some suggestions for how to do that:

- Serve a foster family as they work to help kids without a home.
- Call social services and commit to serve a victim of elder abuse.
- Take in an abused animal.

Lord, I commit to doing something that breaks my heart like it breaks yours.

Signature _____   Date _____

what really matters

The 50-yard field goal that Jordan made as the first half was winding down didn't count because our team didn't get it off in time. All the USC Trojans needed was another second. It was especially disappointing to Jordan because if the field goal had counted, it would have been the longest kick of his career.

As a college kicker Jordan knew that if he missed a kick, his team could lose a game. In college football that could mean the difference between playing in a huge bowl game like the Rose Bowl or going to a less prestigious bowl game. On that misty day in Husky Stadium, his team lost by the same points that had been left on the field when the kick didn't count. By the end of the game, that kick mattered.

What really mattered to Jesus?

To answer that question, Alvin Yoder references Tony Campolo's book *Who Switched the Price Tags?* "Tony says in his book that too often we treat what deserves to be handled with great care as though it was of very little value, and conversely make great sacrifice to do things that have no lasting value. The world's way is to love money and use people to get it. God's way is for us to love people and use money to help others."[11]

We know that children matter to Jesus. He recognized that they probably understood him as well as anybody could. In Matthew 19:14, Jesus said, "Let the little children come to me, and do not hinder them, for the kingdom of heaven belongs to such as these."

Because children matter to Jesus, they should matter to us as well. We have been entrusted with their care to make sure that their basic needs are met and that they aren't exploited.

According to the Consortium for Street Children, no one knows how many street children there are in the world. Estimates have been as high as one hundred million. The true numbers may never be known.[12] We should be appalled by this information. But do the numbers matter? Isn't one child abandoned to his or her fate on the streets of New York, Cairo, or Bucharest one child too many?

Because children matter to Jesus, they should matter to us as well.

It's why I build houses. My ministry started out at an orphanage that took in children from the trash dump. Most had families that loved them but were unable to provide for their basic needs. The orphanage was built to take those families in. After leaving the orphanage, Scott and I started Amor Ministries with a commitment to keep children off the street. We believe that by building homes we do that and more—we keep families together. What matters to Jesus matters to us.

Now let's get back to the game at Husky Stadium. Based on what Tony Campolo said about valuing people and things, do I think that football game really mattered to Jesus? As a USC fan, I believe I know the answer to that. Because if the game had mattered to Jesus, wouldn't the Trojans have won?

OK, football is just a game—of that we can be sure. As much as we have put value on this game that so many of us are passionate about, it's not the kicks or the wins or the stats that matter to Jesus. On the field that day, it was the players who mattered. It's always the people who matter to Jesus.

Disruptive Questions

1. When have you been frustrated with others because what mattered to you didn't matter to them?

2. Make a list of what really matters to you. Now ask yourself which of these items matters most to God.

3. According to the Sermon on the Mount (Matthew 5–7), what are the things that mattered most to God? Read those three chapters to find out what his priorities are.

keep it humble

former board member made a comment about what he loved the most as it related to Amor Ministries. He saw the ministry being committed to diffusing power. That's why we often use this catchphrase when a group comes on a short-term mission trip with us: "It's not about you."

Romans 12:3 says, "For by the grace given me I say to every one of you: Do not think of yourself more highly than you ought, but rather think of yourself with sober judgment, in accordance with the faith God has distributed to each of you." And throughout the Bible we have examples of those who could have used a little dose of humility. In Mark 10:35-40 the apostles James and John were jockeying for position, as they requested seats at the right and left of Jesus on his throne. I just love the response Jesus gave to them when he pretty much put them in their place by asking them if they could do what he could do.

The best part is that they answered with a resounding yes! Jesus went on to tell them that they would get that chance but that the decision concerning who would be granted seats at his right and left was not his to make. Jesus made it clear that those seats will be given "to those for whom they have been prepared."

When I was living at the Tijuana Christian Mission, I had a humbling experience that I continue to draw from when I start to think of myself more highly than I should. I was often called on to speak at various events concerning the ministry of the orphanage. At the young age of twenty-three, this was very flattering. There were moments when I felt a strong sense of self-importance.

On this particular day I was the speaker at a women's luncheon. The agenda was to fellowship over lunch and then retire to a chapel where I would make my presentation. This will definitely date me, but part of my talk involved a slide show. After a short introduction I turned off the lights and took the ladies on a tour of the work I was involved in.

After going through all my slides, I turned on the lights only to discover that every lady in the chapel had dozed off during the talk. Not one of them had heard a thing I said! How humbling to have to admit that on one of my very first speaking engagements, all those in attendance had fallen asleep on me!

Somewhere in this journey, if we're not careful, we can start to think that God is really fortunate to have us on his team. When you go on a short-term mission trip, you need to remember that God was working there before you came and will continue to work there after you have left.

> *Somewhere in this journey, if we're not careful, we can start to think that God is really fortunate to have us on his team.*

When cultivating a mission-focused life, you may be involved in acts of service that are meant to point others to God—not you. As my friend John Fudge says on his Skype message, "There is a God and it's not you." The disciples James and John needed to be reminded of that—and in my opinion that is exactly what Jesus was saying to them.

I challenge you with this parting thought: Don't get so busy serving God that you forget *about* God. When you do that it's really hard to keep it humble.

Disruptive Questions

1. Can you think of a time when you wanted to receive recognition for an act of service? Why was that important to you?

2. Have you ever experienced God's humbling when you were in the midst of serving others? How did that make you feel? What did you learn from the experience?

3. Many people have a hard time allowing others to serve them. When have you let your pride get in the way of letting someone else serve you?

be amor

Just say the name Tim Tebow and you could get a wide variety of reactions. The way he talked about his Christian faith in the NFL was a hot topic in the news in 2011 and beyond. His first year in the league, there were those who wished he would just shut up and play football. And there were others who truly believed he had God on his side—which is why he seemed to be defying the statistical odds and winning games when he was the quarterback of the Denver Broncos.

I don't know Tim Tebow personally, but I think that those who do know him will attest to the fact that he lives what he believes. Through his actions on and off the field and his charity work, he gets what it means to "Be Amor."

I was taken by a statement about Christianity that was made by Apple CEO, the late Steve Jobs. Jobs said, "The juice goes out of Christianity when it becomes too based on faith rather than on living like Jesus or seeing the world as Jesus saw it."[13]

James 2:14-16 puts it this way: "What good is it, my brothers and sisters, if someone claims to have faith but has no deeds? Can such faith save them? Suppose a brother or a sister is without clothes and daily food. If one of you says to them, 'Go in peace; keep warm and well fed,' but does nothing about their physical needs, what good is it?"

So what do I mean when I say "Be Amor"? For me it is about a man who deeply cared for the poor and spent time with prostitutes and tax collectors. It is about Jesus weeping over the city of Jerusalem and physically touching a person with leprosy. Every time I reflect on the Sermon on the Mount (Matthew 5–7) and what those teachings mean for my life, I am reminded of the importance of his love. And Jesus' encounter with the woman at the well (John 4) never fails to take my breath away!

> *For me it is about a man who deeply cared for the poor and spent time with prostitutes and tax collectors.*

How do we live out his message of love today? Our ministry was begun as a way in which we could aspire to be like Jesus and hurt over the things that hurt him. Our commitment was to meet people at their greatest need, and we continue to believe that means providing a home for a family. Actually, we believe it now more than ever! "Being Amor" means working with families in the locations where we serve and keeping those families together.

We believe that preaching the gospel is more than words. Words are necessary, but sometimes our words and actions can contradict each other and undermine the real message. The gospel can lose credibility in those moments, due to our actions, when people look at us and see something other than

Jesus. I believe it could be one of the reasons that led Mahatma Gandhi to say, "I like your Christ; I do not like your Christians."[14] What can we do to change that perspective?

Francis of Assisi gave the challenge, "Preach the Gospel at all times and when necessary use words."[15]

Honestly, I'm more impressed with Tim Tebow's *living* like Jesus than I am when he *talks* about it after a game. But I do believe his words are credible because of the way he lives. The same can be true for us. Wherever God takes you on this journey of a mission-focused life, remember to "Be Amor."

Disruptive Questions

1. Who have you observed that consistently lives out Christ's message of love toward others? What made you choose that person?

2. If others were observing your life (and they are!), where would they see you "Being Amor"?

3. Can you recall a situation that you would like to do over because you weren't "Being Amor"? What happened? What was the effect of that, and what would you do differently?

serving with eyes wide open

Several years ago I heard about a resource that was making some waves in the short-term mission world. David Livermore had written a book that upset quite a few people because they thought he was being critical of short-term missions. I wondered if I should be concerned as well, so I decided to read the book to see what all the fuss was about.

I don't think David was being critical of short-term missions at all in *Serving with Eyes Wide Open*. He was trying to educate people about short-term missions. In order to impact the kingdom on these trips, we must "serve with our eyes open to global and cultural realities so we can become more effective cross-cultural ministers."[16]

Scott and I both went to Mexico the first time while we were in college—but we went to Mexico for different reasons. Scott went down to Tijuana with a group that went shopping, and they simply stopped by an orphanage to help out. I went to visit an orphanage in Tijuana for a weekend and just hung out with the children. We both believed that we were on a short-term mission trip. But we really weren't, not in the way that Livermore defines short-term missions in his book, and not based on what we have learned from over thirty years of experience.

A *Washington Post* writer, Jacqueline L. Salmon, wrote an article titled "Churches Retool Mission Trips." Ms. Salmon talks about a particular church that went to Mexico to build homes and refurbish churches. The pastor of the church was quoted in the article as saying that teens could do just as much good working close by as far away. And their pastor of global engagement stated that the church was repositioning its mission trips "to get away from the vacation-with-a-purpose" mentality.[17]

I agree with both pastors. You can do just as much good working close by as far away. But that isn't the point of serving with eyes wide open. You can do just as much a disservice to the ministry you are serving close by as the one overseas when you don't see the cultural realities of those whom you have gone to serve.

I find it offensive when a mission trip is referred to as a "vacation with a purpose." If you raise support to participate in a short-term mission trip, I hardly believe those supporters would like to know that you are going on a vacation. Oh yeah, with a purpose.

You can do just as much good working close by as far away.

In that *Washington Post* article, Roger Peterson, chairman of the Alliance for Excellence in Short-Term Mission, says, "If [the trips] are only about ourselves, then we're doing nothing more than using another culture . . . to get some benefit at their expense."[18]

When choosing to go on a short-term mission trip, do your research. Wisely choose those whom you will serve alongside, and make sure that what you go to do will help reinforce what they are doing all year long. It will be a win-win for everybody.

Life-Challenging

DISRUPTION

Your life challenge this month is to read David Livermore's book *Serving with Eyes Wide Open*. Then commit to intentionally interact in the lives of immigrants. Here are some practical suggestions for ways to do this:

- Attend a local ethnic fair.
- Attend worship in a language different from your own.
- Attend a religious service you've never been to before.
- Find out if you can volunteer at a local school that has a multi-ethnic population. While you're helping out, you'll be able to observe and learn how parents and children from different cultures interact.

Lord, this month I commit to intentionally
get involved in the lives of immigrants.

Signature _____ Date _____

make it right

We had a guest from England who stayed with us in San Diego after his group returned home. We wanted him to have a Southern California cross-cultural experience, so we . . . took him to Disneyland!

As much as I love the rides, people watching and listening to others are probably the things I enjoy most about being there. Though Disneyland has the reputation for being the "happiest place on earth," you can hear some conversations that aren't happy at all. My favorite is one that I hear probably every time I go there: a mom or dad is shaking the shoulders of a whining or pouting child while saying, "We will have fun here today. I mean it. You are going to have fun!"

As the day was winding down and we were on our way to our last ride, I overheard a conversation that probably everyone in the park could hear. An incredibly loud woman was expressing her anger with someone in her party. She had bought a bottle of soda and had entrusted someone, whom I believe had to be her husband, with carrying it. He had made the mistake of opening it, which (she repeated over and over again) she hadn't given him permission to do.

This woman was mad because she had planned to drink the soda at 10 p.m., and now it would be ruined because he had let out all the carbonation when he opened it at 9 p.m. Got the picture? An explosive outburst of anger at the "happiest place on earth"!

Anger manifests itself in so many ways. If we are too slow to respond when the traffic light changes or if we cut someone off on the freeway, we can become the recipient of vile language or a vulgar gesture. If a checker at a grocery store or a server at a restaurant is slow, or if a waiting line is too long, the result may be outbursts of anger. The woman at Disneyland reminds me of how we spend emotional energy being angry about things that just don't really matter.

There's a story about the great Leonardo da Vinci that speaks to the true spirit of this. It's said that when da Vinci was painting *The Last Supper*, he became angry with someone impeding his progress, and lashed out at him. After that incident, he went back to his painting, but when he reached the point of painting the face of Jesus, he found that he could not do it without first making things right with the person who had caused his anger.

> *The woman at Disneyland reminds me of how we spend emotional energy being angry about things that just don't really matter.*

Regardless of our emotional makeup, anger affects all of us. When we allow anger to control us, we feel bad, knowing that we must make things right.

Ephesians 4:26 challenges us to "go ahead and be angry. You do well to be angry—but don't use your anger as fuel for revenge. And don't stay angry. Don't go to bed angry" (*The Message*).

Paul is communicating at least two thoughts in these verses:

1. There are things that should make us angry.
2. But we shouldn't stay that way.

Cultivating a mission-focused life means making a commitment to being angry about the same things that would make Jesus angry if he were physically walking the earth today. It also means doing something about those things as soon as we can, taking action and committing to making a difference.

I don't believe Jesus wasted anger on anything as unimportant as the loss of carbonation in his Coke bottle, but he did get angry when something mattered. His example challenges us to use our anger to fuel appropriate action.

Disruptive Questions

1. What things made Jesus angry? Read John 8:2-11. Is this one of those situations Jesus should be angry about, and how do you see him making things right?

2. Are you currently angry about anything that you need to make right before you go to bed? What is a tangible action step that you can take today to move toward resolution?

3. What are some things about the world today that you think make Jesus angry?

give voice to
the church

The apostle Paul told Timothy, "Don't let anyone look down on you because you are young, but set an example for the believers in speech, in conduct, in love, in faith and in purity" (1 Timothy 4:12).

Every year during spring I reflect back on this verse. I think about the thousands of young people who cross the border into Mexico during their spring breaks. Some of them come and make complete fools of themselves while a willing media stands ready to show the world how they are acting. And then I think about the thousands of young people who give their spring breaks to serve with us and other ministries in Mexico.

The after-party for each group is so different. One group comes with a total disregard for where they drop their alcohol bottles and trash, leaving the community a mess. The other group comes to build a community of homes, schools, churches, and even a fire station in Rosarito Beach, Mexico—a well-known venue for many of the other spring break parties.

Timothy has been a hero of mine since I was young. I remember the first time I heard about Timothy in the church. I couldn't believe that in the culture in which he lived, he was sent out to minister at such a young age. When I first read the books of Timothy, I was impressed by the tremendous discipline it must have taken to be faithful in his early years. Because *he* seemed to be taken seriously, when I was young *I* very much wanted to be taken seriously as well.

It wasn't until I spoke quite a few years ago on a college campus that I began a real examination of 1 Timothy 4:11, 12. My original intent was to focus the message on the first part of verse 12, where it talks about not letting anybody look down on you because you are young.

Scott and I started Amor in our early twenties, and we have encouraged thousands of students to believe that even though they were young, God could use them to do amazing things. As my friend, the late Mike Yaconelli, said to a group of students around a campfire in Mexico years ago, "Do not let anyone say you are the future of the church; you are the church now! Go home and be the church!"

In the process of studying the text for my series of messages at the college campus, with Mike's words resonating in my mind, I began to ask myself a really important question: Why was Paul willing to entrust Timothy with his own ministry when Timothy was so young?

In verses 11 and 12, Paul challenged Timothy to be strong, to take charge, and to lead. Paul separated authority from seniority. Authority has nothing to do with age or experience. Authority is a reflection of how one conducts his or her life by example and integrity. By how Timothy lived, he had earned that credibility.

Integrity is crucial if we want to be taken seriously—no matter who we are or how old we are. Integrity involves conducting yourself in the same way when others can see you that you would when they cannot.

Christians should be a cut above. The way that we live does affect the kind of voice the church has. We need to raise the standard and have the courage to look one another in the eye and speak the truth in love if our conduct demeans that global voice in any way. We can be a voice of reason in an irrational society, living out the character of Jesus—just like Timothy did. And when we do that, regardless of our age, we are the church.

Disruptive Questions

1. Read 1 Timothy 4 and list the instructions that Paul gave to Timothy as he was preparing him for ministry. How do these specific instructions play into your life?

2. Are you the same person when no one else is watching as you are when you are being watched? Though no one is perfect, through God's Spirit we can learn to rely on his grace and improve in our daily walk with him. How can you make strides to be the person you want to be all the time?

3. What does it look like for you to "be the church"?

giving out of need

Virginia Cooper could spot a moving van a mile away. Of course, that's not so hard when you live on the border of eastern New Mexico and West Texas, one of the flattest places on earth! She seemed to know exactly the moment when the moving van entered the city limits and brought potential members for her little country church.

I'm talking about my mom.

My brothers and I could tell when a new family had moved into our small town, because Mom would begin filling a basket with fresh fruits and vegetables from her garden. She was her own version of Welcome Wagon, and she used this opportunity to invite the new family to join us for worship at First Christian Church.

So it's not a coincidence that I came out of the womb with a missional mind-set. It was the way my family was wired. Whenever a missionary family visited our church, our home was the place where they stayed and had their meals. If some kid in town had been kicked out of his home, my mom was the one who took him in.

Growing up, whenever I came home after an evening out, I

never knew whether my bedroom would already be occupied by someone in need of care. I grew up calling on the sick and elderly with my mom or dad, and I visited my first retirement home when I was eight years old.

Before the word *missional* came into vogue (side note: the term is actually not in some dictionaries), my parents, Bud and Virginia Cooper, lived it. On a daily basis I saw them be generous with what little they had, if it could be used to help someone in need. Generosity was a major part of how they lived out their faith in God.

When I think of my parents and how limited their resources were, it reminds me of the story the Gospel writer told of the widow and her offering: "Jesus sat down opposite the place where the offerings were put and watched the crowd putting their money into the temple treasury. Many rich people threw in large amounts. But a poor widow came and put in two very small copper coins, worth only a few cents" (Mark 12:41, 42).

The best part of this narrative is the explanation Jesus gave to his disciples: "Truly I tell you, this poor widow has put more into the treasury than all the others. They all gave out of their wealth; but she, out of her poverty, put in everything— all she had to live on" (vv. 43, 44).

> *On a daily basis I saw them be generous with what little they had, if it could be used to help someone in need.*

When people send donations to our ministry, they quite often include a note in which they apologize for having so little to give. Yet it is those very same gifts that truly move ministries forward. Sometimes we are embarrassed that we have so little to give, but Jesus made it crystal clear in those verses that he is impressed with "little" gifts.

It's a pretty simple message, and we need to get it. "What can I give?" is not a question of how much. It's much more important to take on the generous spirit of the widow and give just like she did—out of her own need.

Just like Bud and Virginia Cooper.

disruptive questions

1. Have you ever been afraid to give to the church or to a good cause because you didn't trust God to provide for your own needs? When was that, and what caused you to believe that?

2. Do you believe that those with great wealth have been more faithful to God? Why or why not?

3. Maybe you feel like you don't have enough money yourself—or time, clothes, or food. Those things could possibly be what God is asking you to give to others. What are some specific ways in which you can give to others out of your need?

share your possessions

I like these ancient words from a bishop: "If everyone would take only according to his needs and would leave the surplus to the needy, no one would be rich, no one poor, no one in misery."[19]

When I went to live at the orphanage in 1977, I had about fifty dollars a month in support. I had to maintain a car in which I drove kids to school, took teens to their youth activities, picked up people for church, and pretty much did what was asked of me. Then I had to buy my personal items and make payments on a school loan. Yet I have no recollection of ever going without.

What I believed about my possessions was put to the test one day when the orphanage director asked me if I had any money. She was out of milk and was hoping I had the funds to go to the store and buy some. I remember thinking that I had just enough to buy some toiletries that I was running out of. But that money was needed for something else—something more important.

That was probably the day I learned what it truly meant to share my possessions.

I was being asked to give away something I needed because of a greater need. So why did something that seemed to come so naturally for the early Christians now seem so hard for me to understand and live out?

> *That was probably the day I learned what it truly meant to share my possessions.*

In Acts 4:32-35 we read about the believers sharing their possessions:

> All the believers were one in heart and mind. No one claimed that any of their possessions was their own, but they shared everything they had. With great power the apostles continued to testify to the resurrection of the Lord Jesus. And God's grace was so powerfully at work in them all that there were no needy persons among them. For from time to time those who owned land or houses sold them, brought the money from the sales and put it at the apostles' feet, and it was distributed to anyone who had need.

I have heard many Christians attempt to explain the phrase Jesus spoke in Mark 14:7, "the poor you will always have with you." Some young men from the orphanage who were studying for the ministry told me I should quit spending God's money on house building. They quoted this Scripture and said the money would be put to better use if I would give it to them for real evangelism. My understanding of this verse is that our devotion should be to Jesus first—who in turn leads us to the poor. Obviously, the opinions of those young men did not deter us from our calling.

I also believe Jesus' statement reflects his understanding of our nature and a resistance to share our possessions with others. In the story Jesus told in Mark 10:17-31, the rich young ruler was asked to sell all his possessions and give the money to the poor. Ultimately, the rich young ruler decided not to follow Jesus if that was what was required of him.

When Steve Horrex moved from Canada to serve with us in Mexico, he left behind one possession that tied him back to home. His stereo system was the one thing he didn't want to sell—in case this missionary thing didn't work out. A month into his service he received a bill in the mail for his previous year's taxes. It was pretty close to the exact amount he could get for selling that stereo. That was thirty years ago, and you can guess how that turned out!

Wonderful things happen when you follow God's directive to either share or get rid of your possessions.

Life-Challenging

DISRUPTION

Your life challenge this month is to read Acts 1–4. Then commit to live out your faith like someone from the early church. Here are some suggestions for how to do that:

- Sell something and, in Jesus' name, give the money to a needy family in your church or community.
- Within your church or group of friends, have people write down any needs they might have, and then bring those

to the group to see what needs can be taken care of by sharing among yourselves.

- Host a study on the book of Acts, noting how the early church was committed to using what they had in order to meet others' needs.

Lord, this month I commit to living out my
faith like a believer in the early church.

Signature _____ Date _____

choose to celebrate

grew up in a church that was very small, with only about fifty members. Every minister we had was fresh out of Bible college, and it felt like we were the guinea pig for whether or not these young men could make it in the ministry. Honestly, I can't remember any of our ministers' names.

My brother Mitch and I will always remember one couple, because we nicknamed the minister's wife Driller since she was always picking her nose. It was so bad that the elders of the church met with the husband to ask him to get her to stop doing that during the worship service. For some reason I don't think he lasted long in the ministry. (Mitch and I just might have had something to do with that. My mind is a little foggy on that part!)

If the only memories I had of my childhood church were of that minister's wife, you can imagine how dull it might have seemed to me as I grew up. Fortunately, I had other experiences that made church exciting for me, which is why I am still passionate about the church.

When I look at the church of Laodicea that is described in Revelation 3:14-22, I get the feeling that the church wasn't real exciting. Go ahead and read those verses right now. I'll wait. See what I mean? Complacent, lukewarm people are just not real exciting.

Have you ever visited or attended a church that didn't seem to have any fun? Have you ever been on a short-term mission trip that you were glad was short? Over the years Scott and I have visited churches that we would never want to attend. The service was downright boring. The sermon was boring. The people were boring. We couldn't understand why anyone would want to be a part of a church like that. I wonder if that is how people felt about the church in Laodicea.

Even though Amor is not *a* church, we are part of *the* church. We want the people who work here and the people who participate with us on short-term mission trips to feel a sense of celebration in all that we do.

This is most evident each January when the Amor staff travels to our Rancho camp on the border of Tijuana and Tecate to share in worship with our Mexican pastors and their families. At the annual "Dedication of the Season," we share a meal together, and this time of celebration is probably the highlight of our year.

One of Amor's core values is celebration. The value states, "We celebrate working together and purposefully recognize accomplishments throughout the ministry. There is a commitment to celebrate the joyful privilege of using our gifts to make a difference."

As you are reading this book, you are being challenged to cultivate a mission-focused life. If you will commit to listen to God, he will direct your path to a place where you can use your gifts to make a difference. It could be helping with the elderly at a nursing home or tutoring immigrants who don't speak English. Wherever God leads you, choose to celebrate!

In 1993, we took some kids from our inner-city church in

San Diego to come alongside a family in Mexico and, together, build that family's house. Two of the girls on the trip had just recently moved with their family from living in a car to an apartment. I can remember how much impact this trip to Mexico had on them—and how much their response to it had on me.

Instead of feeling sorry for themselves and what they *didn't* have, they celebrated what they had in light of the need they saw in Mexico. Those two girls understood that there were others throughout the world who had it worse than they did— and they were grateful.

In studying the church in Laodicea, we learn that they didn't have an adequate water supply. Interestingly, the church took on the personality of that water supply in being lukewarm. But at least they had water. They had wealth and wool and so many reasons to celebrate.[20]

> *Those two girls understood that there were others throughout the world who had it worse than they did—and they were grateful.*

"Nehemiah said, 'Go and enjoy choice food and sweet drinks, and send some to those who have nothing prepared. This day is holy to our Lord. Do not grieve, for the joy of the LORD is your strength'" (Nehemiah 8:10).

Choose to celebrate today!

Disruptive Questions

1. On the temperature scale, where do you find your faith right now—hot, cold, or lukewarm? Why? What can you do to improve your temperature?

2. Have you ever found yourself like the people in Laodicea—you have everything you need and still are not happy? What is a practical solution for this situation?

3. What are some areas in your life that you can celebrate today? What about family, friends, work, school, or church? Explain your choice.

he is there

E very year on the second Saturday of December, I have two events that I want to attend. If I hurry I can make both, and that includes crossing an international border! These two events couldn't be more different—and yet are so alike. And they remind me of something Augustine said: "God loves each of us as if there were only one of us."[21]

At Solana Beach Presbyterian Church there is a Christmas Tea where women are encouraged to bring a family member or friend and introduce them to the church. As you enter Debin Hall that day and see the beautiful decorations, you can't help but hum the lyric "It's beginning to look a lot like Christmas!"

The tea is a lovely holiday event where tables are set with teacups and saucers brought by those in attendance. A delicious brunch is served by men wearing tuxedos. Everyone dresses in Christmas attire, and I always love looking at the beautiful sweaters that reflect the season. The program is inspiring and causes one to go away with a warm and peaceful feeling.

After the final prayer is uttered, I hurry down the stairs, get in my car, and travel south to Mexico. At the Christmas Tea I make sure I only eat half of what they serve because I'm going to be eating again at our annual pastors' Christmas party. A fiesta of carne asada awaits me, and I've never been one to walk away from tacos with guacamole and salsa!

This party is held at the church of one of our pastors from Baja, and it includes pastors and their families, as well as Amor staff. It has become such a tradition that pastors are starting to bring their grandchildren. The kids all come in their Sunday best with every hair in place.

> *These two events couldn't be more different in how they are carried out, yet they are very much alike in this regard: he is there.*

Before you enter the fellowship hall, you can hear Spanish and the laughter of people having a good time. The tables have paper tablecloths and decorations that have been hand-made with love by the wife of one of our staff members. The food is usually served buffet style on paper plates, followed by games and gifts for the children. The good manners they show in appreciation for everything from a toy to a candy cane never cease to touch my heart.

These two events couldn't be more different in how they are carried out, yet they are very much alike in this regard: *he is there*. Jesus is in attendance at both places.

The tea at Solana Beach Presbyterian gives the women in the church the opportunity to reach out to those who need their lives and hearts changed. The pastors' Christmas party is a celebration of the ministries that do the very same thing throughout the year.

In his song "He Is There," Josiah Brooks asks these questions: "Is there a greater knowledge than to know that he's with us in times of need? Is there anything we can offer to repay the love and sacrifice he gave?"[22]

This is the power of the gospel message: a God who offers himself to us.

Disruptive Questions

1. Have you ever judged those with wealth differently than you judged the poor? When? Do you believe God is more present among one than the other? What makes you say that?

2. Do you think families with means are responsible in part for the condition of the poor? Why or why not?

3. Read Matthew 18:20 and Matthew 28:20. These two passages assure us that Jesus is in the midst of a gathering of believers. What do you think is the evidence that he is there?

great is thy faithfulness

We all have memories of a time and place where something happened that is as vivid as if it occurred yesterday. Some of my memories are so clear that I can even recall what I was wearing that day.

Here's one I will never forget. As Scott and I were driving somewhere, we were discussing a dear friend. I remember saying how you could look up the word *sweet* in the dictionary and you would find her name right there in the definition. And then I turned to Scott and asked a question that will live in infamy for the rest of our lives. I asked Scott if he thought of *me* as sweet.

Any woman reading this will agree that it would have been best for Scott to have answered by just saying, "Yes, honey, I think of you as sweet."

Sitting there I was wondering why it was taking so long for him to answer. In that moment his face went from incredible intensity to such tenderness that when he looked over at me, I really thought he was going to say exactly what I wanted to hear—that my name was right alongside our friend's in the definition of *sweet* in the dictionary.

I'm sure that you have figured out by now that Scott didn't say that he thought of me as sweet. With the kindest voice a wife could wish for, my husband delivered the words I will never forget as long as I live: "Honey, no, I really don't think of you as sweet. I want you to know that I think of you as . . . well, I think of you as thorough."

"What do you mean, I'm *thorough*?!" I screamed at the top of my lungs.

Poor Scott, trying to answer my question honestly yet with a real desire to compliment me, didn't know what had just happened. Our little, yellow Toyota Corolla just became smaller as he was now sitting beside a raving maniac.

> *Some of my memories are so clear that I can even recall what I was wearing that day.*

That particular memory came back to me just recently because of a question that was asked in Mike Yaconelli's book *Messy Spirituality*. The book asks us to consider what we want people to say about us at our funerals. I can tell you right now, I don't want people talking about how thorough I was.

But I do know what I want said. It is what I've always wanted said—that I have been faithful. And when I enter those pearly gates, I am confident that I will hear Jesus say to me, "Well done, my good and faithful servant!" Faithful to my God, faithful to my husband and family, and faithful to the ministry I committed to when I was nine years old.

My favorite hymn is "Great Is Thy Faithfulness," written

by Thomas Chisholm. When Chisholm was asked about his inspiration for writing the hymn, he said he had learned to see the greatness of God. At the age of seventy-five, he wrote, "I must not fail to record here the unfailing faithfulness of a covenant-keeping God and that He has given me many wonderful displays of His providing care, for which I am filled with astonishing gratefulness."[23]

Here's the refrain:

> Great is Thy faithfulness! Great is Thy faithfulness!
> Morning by morning new mercies I see;
> All I have needed Thy hand hath provided—
> Great is Thy faithfulness, Lord, unto me!

The refrain was based on Lamentations 3:22, 23, which exclaims, "Because of the LORD's great love we are not consumed, for his compassions never fail. They are new every morning; great is your faithfulness." When we truly meditate on God's faithfulness, we cannot help but be challenged to be faithful to him.

Disruptive Questions

1. When you think about God's faithfulness to you in the past, what memories come to mind?

2. If you could write your own obituary, what would it say? What do you want people to say about you after you die?

3. What are three ways in which you can be faithful to God today?

on your knees

When I was a young girl, I couldn't wait for missionaries from faraway lands to visit my church. During their presentations I would close my eyes and imagine myself being in their shoes. Their stories of sharing their love for Jesus with people from other cultures moved me to want that for my life someday.

What I remember most vividly about those visits were the stories they told of answered prayers. I loved it when they would talk about God meeting their specific needs in some miraculous way. Time and again they would tell of needing an exact amount of money for a project and someone would send precisely what they had prayed for—down to the exact dollars and cents.

I can remember a family who served in Mexico telling of a time when they needed $86.01 to pay a bill to keep the lights on in their little church. The father shared with us that they barely had enough money for food and that they just didn't know where that other money was going to come from. As a family they got down on their knees and asked God specifically to meet that need for the exact amount. On the day the bill was due, a check in that amount came to them from someone who didn't even know about this need.

Hearing those stories of God answering prayers had a strong impact on me, and it caused me to believe that God listened to *my* prayers and answered them as well. It is also why to this day I pray specifically with confidence. I know that praying not only aligns my heart with God's, but it can transform the lives of others around us.

> *I loved it when they would talk about God meeting their specific needs in some miraculous way.*

Almost twenty years ago in Indianapolis, Indiana, a group of neighbors gathered together to pray for Amy Mathis. It was Amy's third attempt at having a baby, with the previous two being ectopic pregnancies—abnormal pregnancies that occur outside the womb, where the baby cannot survive. The first two times Amy learned of her condition, her husband, Dean, was in Mexico on a short-term mission trip.

The Mathis family was devastated to hear that once again Amy was having an ectopic pregnancy. But they didn't let that deter them from getting a group of neighbors to join them on their knees that weekend, asking God to work a miracle in this situation.

On Monday Amy went to see her doctor. Lo and behold, the baby had moved to the womb! There were some who believed the doctor had made a mistake in the original diagnosis. No, he hadn't. Nine months later the miracle we know as Luke Benjamin was born.

People pray for our ministry in Mexico, and we can feel

those prayers. Friends of mine get together and pray each month for missionaries they know who are working all over the world. Some pray for a country or a specific people group because God has put a burden on their heart.

Many of us pray for people we don't know personally, and who are in places where we will never go, simply as a result of someone bringing us a prayer request.

The Bible says, "I urge, then, first of all, that petitions, prayers, intercession and thanksgiving be made for all people" (1 Timothy 2:1). Prayer is the most powerful resource God has given us, and in his honor we do that on our knees.

Life-Challenging

DISRUPTION

Your life challenge for this month is to read John 11:1-43, where the family of Lazarus was brought to their knees in prayer. Notice how Jesus responded to their prayers.

Reflect on a time when God miraculously answered one of your prayers.

In the spirit of Lazarus's sisters, Mary and Martha, follow up with these practical suggestions for effective prayer on behalf of others.

- Create a prayer calendar for this month that has a daily prayer focus on a particular neighbor and a particular nation.
- Go to Harvest Prayer Ministries (www.harvestprayer. com) and obtain their 64-page prayer guide, *Revolution on Our Knees: Thirty Days of Prayer for Neighbors and Nations*.

- Go to Operation World (www.operationworld.org) and get information under the "Country Lists" tab on how you can pray for specific nations.

Lord, this month I commit to pray daily for my neighbors close by and those serving you in different nations around the world.

Signature _____ Date _____

walking
with god

Enoch is a name you don't hear so often today. At sixty-five years of age, the Enoch in the Bible became a father. He named his son Methuselah, who became the oldest man who ever lived (at least, as recorded in the Bible) at 969 years. We don't hear his name much today either. Most of what we know about Enoch is from the account given in Genesis 5, which concerns the lineage of Adam to Noah. But Enoch's life definitely got God's attention, because he was mentioned in Hebrews 11, the Faith Chapter, where the great men and women of the faith were written about.

Genesis 5:22-24 gives this account: "After he became the father of Methuselah, Enoch walked faithfully with God 300 years and had other sons and daughters. Altogether, Enoch lived a total of 365 years. Enoch walked faithfully with God; then he was no more, because God took him away."

Hebrews 11:5 adds, "By faith Enoch was taken from this life, so that he did not experience death: 'He could not be found, because God had taken him away.' For before he was taken, he was commended as one who pleased God."

In the October 12 devotional of Oswald Chambers's *My*

Utmost for His Highest, we read, "The test of a man's religious life and character is not what he does in the exceptional moments of life, but what he does in the ordinary times, when there is nothing tremendous or exciting on."[24]

If you have just returned from a short-term mission trip, you have more than likely participated in something extraordinary. Maybe you worked alongside a family to build their home or you worked at an orphanage that will take in street children. In that short period of time, you impacted lives in a significant way.

But when you return home, everything that you do can seem ordinary by comparison. Enoch was really just an ordinary man. We don't know much of what he did other than father some children and live to be a really old man. Something we do know about him is that he walked faithfully with God—and evidently God just took him away without his having to die.

How do you walk faithfully with God, after returning home from an earth-shattering, short-term mission trip? Years ago I was speaking at a church, when I was approached by a mom who wanted to share with me what her son said on returning home from his trip with Amor. He said, "Mom, I'm not sure if I'll do anything significant the rest of the year, but that week I went to Mexico and built a house . . . I made a difference."

There is no doubt that this young man made a difference on his short-term trip. What really gets God's attention, though, is what we do with that trip on our return home. We're in a lifelong commitment of walking with God just like Enoch did. Most of the time it feels ordinary, and it might not seem like anything tremendous or exciting is happening.

A friend once had the opportunity to tutor children in a faraway land for a summer. When she returned home, she told me that her tutoring job in the community where she had been working for the last five years now seemed boring. Oswald Chambers said that a person's worth "is revealed in his attitude to ordinary things when he is not before the footlights."[25]

In a remote village that friend of mine had felt like she was in the spotlight. To her it seemed that what she was doing with those children in that village made more of a difference than what she was doing with the children in her own community.

> *What really gets God's attention, though, is what we do with that trip on our return home.*

Then one day a young woman whom she had tutored stopped by her office to let her know that she had been accepted to college and would be the first person in her family to attend. She had come to thank my friend for the role she had played in making that happen. As my friend told me this story, she now recognized that in her "boring program" at home, she had been walking faithfully all along.

And I am sure that God noticed.

Disruptive Questions

1. Have you had any Enochs in your life, men and women who have served the Lord faithfully for years? How has their influence set an example for you?

2. What does walking with God look like after you have returned home from an earth-shattering, life-altering, short-term mission trip?

3. Why do we often want to feel or see the reward of the service that we have done for others?

como estás?

How are you?

I wonder if that question was originally intended to get someone to take the time to hear the answer. Nowadays it always seems buried in a social ritual where it's said just so we *seem* like we care. Maybe we are trying to present an image of kindness but don't genuinely want to know how someone is doing—because that just might ask for some type of commitment from us.

Lately I have wondered whether anyone asked Jesus "How are you?" in those days leading up to the crucifixion—and actually cared about how he was doing. Did Peter, James, or John sit down with him on that final day to find out how Jesus was handling all that was happening to him? Maybe that's why those three were asked to keep watch with him.

But we know how that turned out. We learn in Matthew 26:40 that all three fell asleep. They just couldn't hang with the Son of God. If I am honest with myself, I would have to admit that I probably would have done the same thing. Yes, I would have fallen asleep as well.

What about the lukewarm church in Laodicea that we read about in Week 17? I have an image in my mind that at every service the people probably went through the motions of worship and asked each other in their language, "How are you?"—but didn't really want to know. People who are lukewarm probably don't want to know how you are doing, because you might actually tell them how you are. And that could require them to do something on your behalf.

When you are committed to cultivating a mission-focused life, one of the most beneficial ways to care for others is also the least expensive. And you can do it without going very far. You can ask someone "How are you?" and *listen* for the answer. Sure, it's not as glamorous as going to the jungle to tell indigenous people about Jesus or building an AIDS clinic in Africa. But it's definitely missional.

One of the problems that senior adults deal with most is loneliness, feeling that there aren't people around them who take the time to genuinely listen to them. Here's a sad commentary on this very issue: "Why are the elderly more susceptible and more likely to become victims of a scam? The elderly are vulnerable to scams because they tend to be too trusting, gullible, live alone and don't have someone watching over their finances. Loneliness also plays a role. Elders are often grateful to have someone to talk to—not suspecting that the 'nice man' on the phone may be preying on them."[26]

You can ask someone "How are you?" and listen *for the answer.*

For years First Christian Church in San Francisco served lunch on Christmas Day. One particular year, something quite surprising happened. A limousine pulled up in front of the church, and out stepped a senior citizen who was wearing an expensive fur coat. Having no one to share Christmas lunch with that day, the woman really didn't come for the food. She came because she was lonely. She wanted someone to ask her "How are you?" and mean it.

Making ourselves available to others is exactly what Jesus does for us each day. He genuinely wants to know how we are, and I find him to be a pretty good listener. Wouldn't it be nice if others said that about us?

Disruptive Questions

1. Do you make it a habit to ask someone "How are you?" when you know that you don't really care to listen to the answer? Recall a recent situation when you did that.

2. How does it make you feel when someone asks you a question but doesn't seem to care about your answer?

3. How could you take the time to listen to others in ways in which you haven't in the past? Challenge yourself to intentionally ask someone "How are you?" and then really take time to listen to the response.

the open house

Every fall after the school year is in full swing, parents receive a notice about attending their children's open houses. Teachers have the students clean their desks, and the room is in order for maybe the one and only time during that school year.

As a child, I loved open house night. My parents never missed one that I can remember. It was so much fun to walk in with them and look at my work that the teacher had decided to display. As I think back to those open house nights, I see how my parents' pride and belief in me were part of the reason that I felt confident to succeed in school.

After I had my own family and we moved to San Diego, we decided to have an open house in order to get to know our neighbors. Everyone on the street came. I could tell they were curious about our family because there hadn't been kids in the neighborhood for years. Most of the neighbors had never been in the house, and since a former Mrs. America once lived here, they were excited to see inside.

We met our neighbors at that open house. Food was shared, and long-time residents told stories about families (some nuttier than ours!) who had lived in our house before us. That day we met people from our street who over the years would look out for us and keep an eye on our house when we were away.

In Acts 10 there is the story of a family that had an open house. A Roman centurion by the name of Cornelius invited his relatives and close friends to hear from Peter, one of Jesus' disciples. They heard him speak of how God does not show favoritism but accepts people from every nation who fear him and do what is right. The account in Acts says that after they heard the gospel story of Jesus Christ, they were baptized.

This open house was significant in the life of the early church. Peter was a Jew visiting in the house of an "unclean" Gentile (non-Jew). Such a visit was unheard of in that culture. It showed that God had now granted the Gentiles "repentance that leads to life" (Acts 11:18). Jewish Christians acknowledged that God wanted Gentiles in his family as much as he wanted the Jews.

That day we met people from our street who over the years would look out for us and keep an eye on our house when we were away.

Each of the open houses I have mentioned was unique, and yet all had the same purpose: people were brought together to hear a message. At the open house in the neighborhood school, the message was about how one's child was doing. When we invited the neighbors to our open house, the message was a welcome to the Congdon home. The open house at Cornelius's home was for his family and friends to hear the story of Jesus.

When our family first moved to City Heights in San Diego, we would open our home every Christmas Eve to those who had no place to go and celebrate. A lady who had been attending our church decided to join the church one Sunday, and she gave her testimony about why she had made that decision. Our open house on Christmas Eve had caused her to want to be a part of the church. She explained that she couldn't believe a white family would open their house up to such a diverse group of people.

The message of the open house was that everyone was welcome at the Congdons' and everyone was welcome at Community Christian Church. That was the same message people heard that day in the house of Cornelius.

What does your open house quotient look like?

Disruptive Questions

1. What message do you send to your neighbors about your house? In what ways do you send out that message?

2. Do you feel that your church is an open house or a closed house? What makes it that way?

3. Are there certain people groups that your church (or your family) has been guilty of shunning? What can you personally do to help the situation?

in our backyard

I wish I had a dollar for every time I've been asked this question: "Why are you helping the people in Mexico when we have so many needs in our own country?" When we were living in our first apartment, an anonymous neighbor sent us a note with that very question written on it.

Our offices for the ministry were on the campus of Pacific Christian College in Fullerton, California, located just thirty-two miles from Los Angeles (which has the second largest population of Latinos in the world). I began asking myself a different question: "Why can't we do both? What's keeping us from ministering abroad as well as in our own backyard?"

Our family made a commitment that we would do both. And that is why, in 1989, we moved our ministry offices to the border of Mexico and our family to City Heights, a racially diverse urban community in San Diego, California. We wanted to live in a place where we could minister not only in Mexico but also in our own backyard.

A group of us moved as part of a church-planting team, with a belief that we should live in the neighborhood with the people we were asking to come to church. One of the first families to come to Community Christian Church was the Henderson family. The late Susan Henderson told me many times that the reason she and her son decided to be a part of the church was that we were her neighbors. She was tired of feeling like Christians drove in from the suburbs and wanted to help, but were not truly invested in the community.

As we invested our lives in this community, relationships were built that continue to be a part of our lives today. Since we didn't have a building to meet in, our home became the place to meet—especially our backyard. I can remember our first Halloween with over fifty kids bobbing for apples, some for the first time in their lives.

Christmas Eve services and an Easter egg hunt were also held in our backyard. The youth group had their weekly Bible study and countless activities there. Even the local high school basketball team held their pregame meals in our backyard for one season.

> *What's keeping us from ministering abroad as well as in our own backyard?*

When we finally had a church building, I performed the wedding of a young woman who had grown up in our church. That November evening Scott, Jordan, and I hosted her reception . . . where else? In our backyard.

There isn't a time that I go into our backyard when one of the memories of ministry through the years doesn't come to mind. It is something that usually brings a laugh because so many of the images I have of those times were downright hilarious!

Over lunch with a friend, I asked how she and her family had gotten involved in an inner-city project in their area. She said that after they had returned from a short-term mission trip to a country that reflected some of the diversity in that nearby neighborhood, she told her husband that they needed to do something in their own backyard. Isn't it amazing that after we return from a short-term trip, we see the needs in our own backyard that we had missed before the trip?

Life-Challenging

DISRUPTION

Your life challenge for this month is to ask yourself: "Do I know my neighbors?" Then commit to planning and organizing an activity for the people in your neighborhood. Here are some practical suggestions for how to do this:

- Organize a potluck dinner (or dessert and coffee) at your house.
- Consider hosting a weekly backyard Bible club for the kids in your neighborhood. Get the teenagers involved by having them help with crafts and sports.
- Do a neighborhood VBS for one week in the summer in your backyard. Get kids and adults in your community serving others with Standard Publishing's VBS, *God's Backyard Bible Camp—Under the Stars* (025497113) or *God's Backyard Bible Camp—Under the Sun* (025497013). Learn more at www.vacationbibleschool.com.

Lord, this month I commit to plan and organize an
activity for the people in my neighborhood that
will bring them into my home or backyard.

Signature _____ Date _____

give them
dignity

Growing up, I was what you would call a Vacation Bible
School junkie. In the '60s, we didn't have all kinds of
camps that parents could enroll their children in for the
summer, as they do today. We pretty much had to create our
own fun, and that wasn't all bad. Each summer I attended
VBS at as many churches as I could find. I especially loved
the VBS program at my neighbors' church. They had the best
crafts and snacks—plus you got two breaks to go outside and
play.

In the '60s, we girls had to wear skirts to church. But on
the playground you could wear your shorts. One particular
summer the cool thing was to wear shorts under your skirt.
That allowed you to make the most of your playground time
by just taking off your skirt instead of having to go into the
restroom and change into shorts.

I remember the Wednesday of one particular VBS as if it
were yesterday. Everyone was hurrying to get outside, and as
I was running I decided to pull down my skirt with the elas-
tic waistband. Yep, more than my skirt came down that day
in front of about two hundred kids. At that moment I was

embarrassed; I had lost my dignity. Needless to say, that was my last day at that VBS. I don't think I ever went back to that church.

Throughout the ministry of Jesus, we see him giving people their dignity. Whether it was a blind person or a person with leprosy, the fatherless and widows, or women and children, he gave people a sense of their own worth and value.

> *Throughout the ministry of Jesus, we see him giving people their dignity.*

Since the beginning of time, the human race has ascribed dignity to people and things that are in direct contrast to where God would place it. In the case of David, the nation of Israel didn't really value David, but it was God's decision to make him king. In 1 Samuel 2:8 we see the evidence of God's viewpoint: "He raises the poor from the dust and lifts the needy from the ash heap; he seats them with princes and has them inherit a throne of honor. For the foundations of the earth are the LORD's; on them he has set the world."

Dean Mathis has his own dignity story. When I was living at Tijuana Christian Mission, Dean often would lead a group of students from Pacific Christian College in Fullerton, California, to help out our ministry at the Tijuana dump. Dean was the photographer of the group and was always looking for the photo that would impact people the most when he showed them what the students were doing in Mexico.

On one particular trip to the dump, he turned a corner and saw the picture he couldn't wait to capture.

A father was crouching down over a bucket of slop, and with a spoon in his hand, he was feeding his baby boy what others had thrown away. As Dean started to take the photo, the father turned to him and looked him straight in the eye. Dean knew he couldn't take this photo. He also knew that the image would be imprinted in his mind forever.

This father deserved to have the dignity of feeding his child without anyone else seeing how he had done that. Dean Mathis turned away and gave that father the dignity he deserved.

I think Jesus would have done the same.

Disruptive Questions

1. In what specific ways did Jesus give people dignity? (See Matthew 8:1-4; John 5:1-15.)

2. Have you ever felt like your dignity was taken away by another person? What happened? How did you feel?

3. In an act of service on a short-term mission trip or a local outreach, have you thought that maybe what you were doing took away dignity from those you were serving? If so, how could you have served differently? How will this help you in future service outreaches?

the kindness of strangers

The last line from Tennessee Williams's *A Streetcar Named Desire* is "I have always depended on the kindness of strangers."[27] I can just imagine that is how the man traveling from Jerusalem to Jericho in the parable of the Good Samaritan must have felt after being beaten, robbed, and left for dead (Luke 10:30-37).

The injured man maybe never knew that two professional religious workers, a priest and a Levite, not only passed him by but had moved to the other side of the road to avoid him. So much for the kindness of strangers.

In the parable that Jesus told, a stranger from an unlikely place, Samaria, helped a Jewish man that day on the side of the road. This was an out-of-the-ordinary act of kindness by a Samaritan for a Jew. It was not normal, because the Jews believed that the Samaritans were unclean, and they would have nothing to do with them. What great kindness was shown that day by a man who was looked down on by the very one he would serve!

I recall traveling alone from Nice, France, to Luton, England. I got on the plane and took my typical seat closest to the restroom. I sat down, opened my Kindle, and began reading until the flight attendant would tell me to turn it off. I normally get lost in the adventure of what I'm reading and don't notice the commotion around me before takeoff. On this particular day there was unusual commotion as a gentleman was being asked to leave the plane and he was looking through all the overhead bins for his suitcase.

Scott often tells me I should be more aware of my surroundings, and as far as that day was concerned, he was right. Before I knew it, the man opened the bin above me and pulled out his suitcase. All I remember is being hit very hard on the head with the suitcase. I woke up to someone who looked like a rugby player asking me, "Are you OK?"

But what happened after that reminded me of the parable in Luke about the Good Samaritan. A complete stranger, very likely from Britain, reached over and took my hand and asked if I was OK and if I needed any help. He gave me a tissue to wipe my tears as I cried over the pain caused by the impact of that 30-pound suitcase. And throughout my whole flight he was there taking care of me. At that moment I was living the last line from *A Streetcar Named Desire*, as I was depending on the kindness of that stranger.

Each June, as part of the Amor Family Camp, families descend on Mexico from all over the United States. Many houses are built by those families—a tangible demonstration of kindness by a group of strangers. I believe when so many people are passing by our neighbors in Mexico (moving to "the other side" of the road), those who do come to help are, in the truest sense of this parable, Good Samaritans.

Also in Luke 10, a discussion took place between Jesus and a man who was an expert in the law. Jesus asked the man what was written in the law about receiving eternal life, and the man's answer in verse 27 was to "Love the Lord your God" and to "Love your neighbor as yourself." The man then asked Jesus, "Who is my neighbor?"—which was the perfect setup for Jesus' story of the Good Samaritan.

A complete stranger, very likely from Britain, reached over and took my hand and asked if I was OK and if I needed any help.

I believe our neighbors are those who need our help, those who are desperately depending on the kindness of strangers. May we not "pass by" them but always live the life of a Good Samaritan. Remember Jesus' words: "'Which of these three do you think was a neighbor to the man who fell into the hands of the robbers?' The expert in the law replied, 'The one who had mercy on him.' Jesus told him, 'Go and do likewise'" (vv. 36, 37).

Disruptive Questions

1. Have you ever been the recipient of the kindness of a stranger? What happened?

2. Have you ever walked away from an opportunity to be a Good Samaritan? What happened? What did you learn from that experience that may help you in the future?

3. Based on the story in Luke 10, what do you think it really means to love your neighbor as yourself? How do you (or how can you) live that out on a daily basis?

the least
of these

Why is it that some people with money or power try to use it to get their way, no matter who it hurts? My friend and mentor, the late pastor Bill Miles, introduced me to Harry, a member of Bill's church in San Francisco. Harry was a '60s product of the Haight-Ashbury district, where people dropped acid and literally burned out their brains.

Unfortunately, Harry was one of those flower children who couldn't remember where he came from or even if Harry was his real name. When I met him he walked with the help of a cane and wore a headband that looked like an American flag around his long, shaggy, gray hair.

But I had a real crush on him. He was the greeter at the church. And during the question-and-answer period after I preached a sermon, Harry seemed to be the one person who understood what my message was all about. It really tickled me that a burned-out hippie was who I connected with most at that inner-city church. This goes to prove that God really does have a sense of humor.

A particular couple (who just happened to put the most

money in the Sunday offering) felt that visitors to the church were turned off by Harry. After one Sunday service they told Bill that the church would never grow as long as Harry was a member. And they added that it would be better for him to leave.

Then they issued Bill and the church leaders an ultimatum: either Harry had to go or they were going to leave, taking with them their generous offerings. As you can imagine, tempers flared over the situation, so Bill told everyone to calm down, go home, and think about it. He asked the leaders to take a week and reflect on what had been said and pray for guidance on what to do.

For one elder in the church, it was pretty clear. Over the years he had heard Pastor Miles preach a simple message about "whatever you did for one of the least of these brothers and sisters of mine, you did for me" (see Matthew 25:31-46). Every time that elder listened to Bill's favorite message, he knew that Harry was exactly who Jesus was talking about.

> *Every time that elder listened to Bill's favorite message, he knew that Harry was exactly who Jesus was talking about.*

A decision was made. The leaders at First Christian Church would rather be sheep than goats.

This Matthew 25 parable Jesus told about the least of these is compelling because it uses the images of these two animals to convey the difference between those who get it and those who don't.

These verses in Matthew reveal how those Jesus referred to as the sheep respond to people in need. They give food to the hungry and drink to those who thirst. They clothe the naked and invite strangers into their homes. Caring for the sick and visiting those in prisons aren't options for anyone who wants to be a reflection of God's commitment to the least of these.

The elder was right. Jesus was represented in the person of Harry, who was "one of the least of these."

Disruptive Questions

1. Read Matthew 25:31-46. Why do you think some people in this passage were able to love "the least of these" but others could not?

2. Of the different groups of people mentioned in the parable of the sheep and the goats, (such as the hungry, thirsty, those in prison), which group is hardest for you to serve? Why?

3. Are there situations in which you find yourself sounding like the couple who wanted Harry to leave? What can you do to change your attitude?

love your neighbor as yourself

In the summer of 1976, a busload of children from the Tijuana Christian Mission came to stay for a weekend in the dorms at Pacific Christian College, where I was a student. They were going to visit Knott's Berry Farm. The trip had been coordinated by a college girl, a good friend of mine, who was doing her summer internship at the orphanage.

That weekend I fell in love. With San Juana and Choppo, Enrique and Israel. I was a goner. On several occasions I had resisted going to Mexico with my fellow classmates. Honestly, it just didn't interest me. That was until I met those children.

As I have said before, I actually went kicking and screaming on my first visit to the orphanage. But the clincher was when my friend dangled in my face the opportunity to see those children again. The rest is history. That weekend I crossed the border and began a journey that would teach me what Jesus meant when he told us to love our neighbors as ourselves.

One of the teachers of the law . . . asked him, "Of all the commandments, which is the most important?"

"The most important one," answered Jesus, "is this: 'Hear, O Israel: The Lord our God, the Lord is one. Love the Lord your God with all your heart and with all your soul and with all your mind and with all your strength.' The second is this: 'Love your neighbor as yourself.' There is no commandment greater than these" (Mark 12:28-31).

That weekend I fell in love. With San Juana and Choppo, Enrique and Israel.

A youth pastor once told me of her son's commitment to choose a mission trip over his sports activity. He was willing to turn in his high school soccer jersey to his coach because the coach had told her son that if he went to Juárez over spring break and missed practice, he would be kicked off the team.

How can people say this generation isn't committed to anything? That young man loved his neighbor more than he did himself.

Mike Farra has been one of the most proficient disrupters I have ever known. One of the ways he has done that was to take his youth group on trips where they usually departed at midnight instead of during daylight. He wasn't afraid to take his students on mission trips where no one else would go.

Mike took this to another level one summer at Angeles Crest Christian Camp. He led three hundred high school students that week through Matthew 25 with a focus on the rich and the poor. One of the exercises he did with these students was meant to teach them not to just love their neighbors, but to love them as much as they loved themselves.

Mike directed the campers to go to their cabins and find a piece of clothing to donate. When the students returned to the hall, they were led through a discussion on how they felt about giving up one of their possessions. Most of the campers said that if they had known they were going to be giving a piece of clothing to the poor, they would have brought something they didn't want anymore. But that's not loving your neighbor as yourself, is it? And don't poor people want something nice just like you do?

This lesson challenged the students to do for others the same things that they would do for themselves. Mike told me that this exercise had an even greater effect than he could have expected. In the end the campers were ready to give all they had to the poor.

I think the toughest part of Jesus' command to love our neighbors is the challenge to love them "as yourself." But unless you can do that, have you really loved your neighbor?

Life-Challenging

DISRUPTION

Your life challenge this month is to read Matthew 25:31-46 and seek practical ways in which it applies to your life. Then commit to evaluate your resources and sacrifice something in order to serve the kingdom of God. Here are some hands-on suggestions for how to do that:

- Give away a favorite item of clothing to a program that helps people who are trying to get back on their feet. Who knows—your clothing might be worn by someone going on a job interview or by a child whose parent has lost his job! Invite your friends to join in and give away clothes as well.
- Find a place to serve alongside people who will cause you to assess how you look at and evaluate others. Challenge yourself to serve somewhere you wouldn't normally think about going. For instance, I taught English as a second language to Korean people. With no experience in that culture, I was initially intimidated. But I grew to love them and their culture just as I had the people in Mexico and in my own inner-city community.

Lord, this month I commit to evaluate my resources and sacrifice something in order to serve the kingdom of God. I want to learn to serve those who may be a challenge for me.

Signature _____ Date _____

sharing the good news

Are you one of those totally together people who sends out a family update along with your Christmas cards every year? Do you manage to have those in the mail the Monday after Thanksgiving? If you are someone who does that, then I really admire you! I not only don't put together a holiday letter; I can't recall ever sending out a Christmas card. But I love getting them, because I look forward to hearing about family and friends and seeing pictures of how the kids have grown.

Wouldn't you have loved to read Mary's first holiday letter after Jesus was born? I wonder what she would have written as she tried to explain to family and friends what had happened in the life of their family that past year. An update on her cousin Elizabeth would have been interesting! And the pictures would have been amazing (see Luke 1:39-45).

Mary and Elizabeth weren't able to put together an impressive holiday letter with computer graphics and photoshopped pictures, but they would have wanted to share their good news. I'm sure these two women wanted everyone to know that God had blessed them with boys who were special.

They aren't much different than any of us who are parents. Whether it's a holiday letter or not, we love news—hearing it and sharing it with family and friends.

A family in Puerto Peñasco, Mexico, had lost their house in a fire. With no place to live, they were taken in by members of one congregation. And that Mexican church made a commitment to build them a new home if Amor could provide the materials.

Stepping out on faith we told the pastor to set a date to build, as we had already received some monies to put toward the building of a house in Puerto Peñasco. A humble group of people from the church built a new house, and the family in need worked right alongside.

Through the generosity of some of our donors who responded to this family's story, we received all the funds needed to build this home.

Whether it's a holiday letter or not, we love news— hearing it and sharing it with family and friends.

So what would that family have to say in their holiday letter, if they had written one? My hope would be that they would tell of the good message being preached to them through the love of that church in Puerto Peñasco that took them in during their time of need. And that they would believe the good news as it was preached to them through the building of their home.

Ultimately, my hope would be that this family would tell

how they had been sent to preach the good news to another family in need—a family just like them.

"How, then, can they call on the one they have not believed in? And how can they believe in the one of whom they have not heard? And how can they hear without someone preaching to them? And how can anyone preach unless they are sent? As it is written: 'How beautiful are the feet of those who bring good news!'" (Romans 10:14, 15).

Have you shared the good news of Jesus recently?

Disruptive Questions

1. If you had been Mary, what would you have told people that your son was here to do?

2. In what ways do you share your news with family and friends? Through Facebook, texting, Skype, Christmas cards, e-cards, or by some other means? What kinds of news do you get most excited about?

3. What is your good news story of how you came to Jesus? How can you share that with family and friends in the near future in a practical way?

what are you going to do?

Mary-Lou Weisman made the following humorous observation about retirement:

> In the beginning, there was no retirement. . . . In the Stone Age, everyone was fully employed until age 20, by which time nearly everyone was dead, usually of unnatural causes. Any early man who lived long enough to develop crow's-feet was either worshiped or eaten as a sign of respect. Even in Biblical times, when a fair number of people made it into old age, retirement still had not been invented.[28]

Retirement in the United States is a fairly new concept; it has only been around for about the past sixty years. Studies have shown that as older people face death, one of their regrets is that they didn't do more for others. They didn't volunteer enough.

On *The Chicago Cares Blog,* the question is raised, "Plenty of people regret that they didn't do more, but have you ever met someone who wished that they had done less?"[29]

That's a great question.

Moses didn't retire. As a matter of fact, he worked up until the day he took his last breath. Deuteronomy 34:5-7 says, "And Moses the servant of the Lord died there in Moab, as the Lord had said. He buried him in Moab, in the valley opposite Beth Peor, but to this day no one knows where his grave is. Moses was a hundred and twenty years old when he died, yet his eyes were not weak nor his strength gone." His life counted up until the very end.

In December 2003, my dear friend Jeanette Arthur made the decision to retire after working almost nineteen years in the newspaper world, because she no longer wanted to work seventy to eighty hours a week. What was she going to do now that she was no longer working full-time?

Since walking away from the daily grind, how she chose to serve others is an example to everyone who wonders what they are going to do upon retirement. Through an organization called Childhelp, Jeanette has made a significant difference in the lives of children who are victims of abuse and neglect. Here is their mission statement: "Childhelp® exists to meet the physical, emotional, educational, and spiritual needs of abused, neglected and at-risk children. We focus our efforts on advocacy, prevention, treatment, and community outreach."[30]

Jeanette has served this organization in a wide variety of ways, but the greatest impact that I have seen is her commitment to Childhelp's Special Friends program. Because these children have limited one-on-one attention, the Special Friend is able to spend quality time with that child and make him or her feel special, sometimes for the first time in the child's life.

The minimum requirement is to make three visits and then send cards a couple of other times during the year.

Jeanette has done that and more. She took her Special Friend into her life and into her heart. And both their lives were transformed.

Jeanette's first Special Friend was the youngest of fourteen siblings, with no known parents. He struggled academically and even seemed afraid to get out of the car when they went to McDonald's. Jeanette remembers that it was six months before he was able to look her in the eyes.

Jeanette was able to reach into the depths of this abused and neglected little boy and bring out of him all the love that God had put inside his little heart. And this all happened because Jeanette knew when she retired that there was something better for her to do.

All of us can learn from Jeanette's example of what it means to have a life that we can look back on with no regrets. And that's a life from which you'll never retire, until God calls you home to be with him.

Disruptive Questions

1. If you're old enough to think about retirement, what kind of dreams have you had concerning your future? If this is still a long way off for you, what kinds of career plans do you have?

2. Are you living with any regrets? If so, what are they? What can you do to remedy the situation?

3. Where are some places you could serve—and what kinds of things could you do there—that would fulfill the dreams you have?

no greater love

ove is an interesting word. It can often be a word we just say, with very little meaning behind it. When I lived in Mexico right after college, I didn't know a word of Spanish. My best friend at the orphanage where I lived, Neri, started teaching me phrases and told me that she used *te quiero mucho* when she wanted to express her deep love and care for someone. She said that the use of *yo te amo* (I love you) had become an easily tossed around phrase in Spanish.

A disrupted life is one that loves like Jesus did when he laid down his life for us. He explains it this way in John 15:9-13: "As the Father has loved me, so have I loved you. Now remain in my love. If you keep my commands, you will remain in my love, just as I have kept my Father's commands and remain in his love. I have told you this so that my joy may be in you and that your joy may be complete. My command is this: Love each other as I have loved you. Greater love has no one than this: to lay down one's life for one's friends."

It takes deep love and care to lay down one's life for one's friends. That's what Jesus did and what he has called us to do. And that's what Neri did for me one day on the streets of Tijuana, Mexico.

I was twenty-three years old and living at Tijuana Christian

Mission. Neri, the sister of the orphanage director, was living upstairs and attending university—studying to become a teacher. One day Neri and I had to run an errand at the Bible college. As we got out of the car, a man grabbed my leg and wouldn't let go. I'm not sure what he was planning, but I knew it wasn't good.

Neri came flying around the car, and believe me when I say that was no easy task! She was five feet tall and weighed about 250 pounds, but her body moved like a gazelle that day. Before I knew it, that man had been knocked to the ground and his nose was bloodied. Neri and I were already very close friends, but that situation gave us a special bond as I saw her live out this passage in John that day on the streets of Tijuana.

Those pastors genuinely live out daily John 15:13 and te quiero mucho.

Te quiero mucho—that deep love and care—motivates our pastors in Juárez to continue serving a city where thousands of people have left as a result of the violence there. Those pastors genuinely live out daily John 15:13 and *te quiero mucho*.

Javier and Rosy Heredia Rodriguez pastor Templo Puertas del Cielo in Ciudad, Juárez. Every Friday Rosy and a group of women from that church make burritos and take them to the hospital in Juárez. They aren't allowed in, so they stand outside, rain or shine, and give the food to the families who are seeing their loved ones (many of whom have been caught in a web of violence associated with the drug cartel), sometimes for the last time.

I asked if it was dangerous to be there. She said that of course it was. But the opportunity to give a burrito in the name of Jesus to those who have possibly been the cause of violence in their city hasn't deterred these women who virtually have nothing themselves. They are living out John 15:13 and *te quiero mucho*.

Cultivating a mission-focused life means that in spite of the many challenges, we continue to serve. Whether it is to those associated with the drug cartel who are outside a hospital in Juárez or putting yourself in danger while protecting your friend on the streets of Tijuana, there is no greater love!

To whom can you demonstrate *te quiero mucho* today?

Disruptive Questions

1. Have you ever laid down your life for a friend? If yes, what happened? If no, what would motivate you to do so?

2. Who are the strangers in your life whom you find hard to love? Following the example of Rosy and her friends, what could you do to change that?

3. So maybe your gift isn't making burritos. What could you distribute to others in Jesus' name?

let me be
your witness

Witness is not just a little activity we do now and again. Witness is who we are," says Darrell L. Guder, editor of *Missional Church*. "The world will encounter God's love in Christ . . . because Christians are equipped by God's Spirit using Scripture to demonstrate the truth, the relevance, the healing power of the gospel."[31]

We can look to Isaiah 58:7 for the witness that Guder is talking about: "Is it not to share your food with the hungry and to provide the poor wanderer with shelter—when you see the naked, to clothe them, and not to turn away from your own flesh and blood?"

When I was disrupted by Christ, this witness of living out the gospel message was manifested in my very young life. A boy named Perry sat right behind me in my third-grade class. Perry was raised by a single dad because his mom had abandoned their family (which included Perry and his three brothers). Perry and I became fast friends.

I really felt sorry for my classmate. He sometimes came to school without shoes, and he didn't seem to have a winter coat. My family was not well off, but my brothers and I had our basic needs met. We had food on our table and a roof over our heads. Even though I wasn't in the most current fashion, I had good shoes and a sturdy coat to keep me warm when the wind blew across the plains of eastern New Mexico.

Sometime during that year I began to notice that Perry usually didn't have much for lunch, and some days had nothing at all. So I took it on myself to bring extra food in my brown bag to share with Perry. That's living a mission-focused life, right?

> *I confessed I had been taking the food.*

However, there was a slight problem in my effort to share food from the Cooper cupboard. I hadn't bothered to ask Mom's permission before zipping off to school on my bike each morning with twice as much food as I needed. So one evening I was beckoned into our family room, along with my brothers, for a meeting with our mom to investigate which of us kids was eating her "out of house and home," as she put it.

After some significant finger pointing and my brothers putting me in the dreaded scissors lock, I confessed I had been taking the food. As you can imagine, Mom wasn't happy with me; but when she heard the reason, she was proud of her "little missionary"!

I do believe Perry encountered God's love in a brown lunch bag that year. And it was because his classmate's life had been disrupted and she was now living a mission-focused life.

Life-Challenging

DISRUPTION

This month's life-challenging disruption focuses on Isaiah 58 and the commitment to true fasting. Read that chapter in preparation for making an agreement with God to make a sacrifice that will free up resources—time and money—to give to those in need of food. Some sources say that 800 million people in the world are chronically hungry. Others estimate that a billion people eat only one-third or one-half cup of rice a day.[32] Here are some action steps to consider:

1. How many times do you grab coffee, fast food, or a meal in a restaurant? Give up those items for one week this month—it will be a fast from convenience. When you long for the easy access to what you want, use those moments to focus on the issues of hunger throughout the world, asking God to open your eyes to those around you.

2. Once a week this month—either on your own, with a group, or with your entire family—eat what amounts to an average meal for those who hunger: one-third of a cup of rice or beans. Use this mealtime to consider or discuss issues of hunger throughout the world. As hunger begins to hit you, remember that you cut down only one meal for the week. For many, this would be their usual meal for the day.

3. If possible, fast for an entire day and feel the pain of hunger in your stomach. Notice how it affects your thinking ability. This is only one day for you. Consider those who are born into poverty and know nothing but the pain of an empty and bloated stomach.

Now take the money you saved and make a difference. With your group, family, or interested friends, decide how you will give that money to a local food bank or to a ministry with a food program. Then do it.

You can take it a step further. Raise awareness and involvement in your community in one of these ways:

- Take time to volunteer at the local soup kitchen or food bank where you have made your financial donation.
- Organize a food drive through your church and go door-to-door asking your neighbors for dry or canned food that can be given to a local church or ministry that helps neighbors in need.
- Ask your neighborhood schools if they need donations for hungry kids, and donate something.
- Volunteer to make and deliver holiday food bags for local families.
- Make food deliveries for groups who take food to shut-ins.

You might discover a passion for serving God in this way. You may also develop relationships with those you have come alongside. Hunger is a worldwide issue, and you can make a commitment now to be a part of the solution, wherever you are.

> Lord, this month I vow to sacrifice one meal a week
> to give to your people in need.
>
> Signature _____ Date _____

serving together

W hen Joshua challenged God's people, he declared, "Choose for yourselves this day whom you will serve. . . . As for me and my household, we will serve the LORD" (Joshua 24:15).

Neither of my parents is alive. Since losing my mom and dad, I have had time to reflect on all the things they did that were good. Both had tough upbringings, and yet they did a lot of things right. One of those things was that my brothers and I knew that our family was what mattered most.

My parents made church involvement a priority, and church activities were the cornerstone of our family life. Some of my favorite memories from childhood were occasions when we served the church together as a family. I can remember the times our family drove to the Guadalupe Mountains so that we could help build the church camp I attended as a kid. A few years back I spoke at that camp. It was doubly nostalgic because it's also the place where I'd made a commitment to be a missionary.

Families weren't really going on short-term mission trips much back when I was a kid, but I had a lot of exposure to missionaries. It was just a given that when missionaries visited our church, they would be guests in the Cooper home.

Together as a family we would serve my mom's home cooking and provide warm beds.

In his book *Ordering Your Private World*, Gordon MacDonald talks about making memories instead of accumulating things. That is why we created Mexico Family Camp. Scott, Jordan, and I—along with Dean, Amy, Luke, and Joel Mathis—did this because we believe there is no better way for a family to make memories than by sleeping in a tent in Mexico and building a house together.

> *My parents made church involvement a priority, and church activities were the cornerstone of our family life.*

In the book *Trained in the Fear of God*, Michael S. Wilder wrote a chapter titled "Building and Equipping Missional Families." He asks, "How, at a practical level, can families develop a clear vision for how they will be used in God's service and mission?" He suggests creating a family mission statement and gives this guideline, which we've abbreviated, for how to get that process going:

- Discuss your values. Ask your family what is most important to each of them and record the answers.
- Evaluate your values. Ask your family to evaluate each response in light of Scripture.
- Compose your family mission statement.
- Make a family commitment. Work with the entire family to memorize the family mission statement.
- Establish a game plan. . . . [Plan and set] goals to

implement the mission statement in specific ways in daily living.[33]

Even if everyone in the family does not have the same beliefs, it is important for the family to have a common goal. Serving together will help that goal become a mission.

When we look at the children of Israel as a nation, as well as the individual families that made up that nation, we see that many of their problems were a result of divided households. Jesus offered this challenge: "Every kingdom divided against itself will be ruined, and every city or household divided against itself will not stand" (Matthew 12:25). That is why Amor's mission is to build homes with families so that they can keep their families together. We refer to our Mexico Family Camp as "families building homes and homes building families!"

Disruptive Questions

1. What are some of your personal core values? What are your most important values as a family?

2. How are you doing in regard to making memories instead of accumulating things? What changes could you make to weight it more on the making memories side?

3. What would it take for you to commit to planning a short-term mission trip at home or abroad with your family? What barriers do you need to remove? Can you plan to make a timetable to work toward this goal?

money made was put back into the program to improve on it for the next year.

To teach your children well, I believe that you have to challenge them to use their gifts and talents to make a difference in the world. Then get out of the way and let God raise your children to be all he wants them to be!

························
Disruptive Questions

1. If you are a parent, what goals do you have for your kids as they grow up? If you are a teen or young adult, what do you aspire to be, based on God's desire for your life? How can you pursue God in your life choices?

2. If you are a parent, what are the values you model and teach your children about serving others? If you are a teen or young adult, what values were modeled for you by your parents? How can you pass those values on to future generations?

3. As a family or as an individual, what are some ways in which you can model and teach a servant attitude to those beyond your family circle?

give them to the lord

My dad passed away in 2005. Yet I often reach for the phone, wanting to hear one of his famous one-liners that could make me laugh so hard I cried. I miss him, and even now just reflecting back on him causes tears to well up in my eyes.

In the summer of 1977, I made a call to my parents that I know just broke my dad's heart. I was in Yuma, Arizona, representing Tijuana Christian Mission at a Vacation Bible School. My friend, Laretta Shrader, told me to go ahead and take all the time I needed to talk with my mom and dad on her house phone about the decision I had made to go live in Tijuana, Mexico.

Upon hearing my announcement, my dad was stunned, to say the least. I do remember raised voices on both sides. He was not happy that I wasn't using my newly acquired college degree to go out and get a job and provide for myself. And I know he felt helpless when I told him that I sensed God was calling me to go work at the orphanage that I had been visiting each weekend during my senior year at Pacific Christian College.

So how do you think I reacted the day my son, Jordan, wanted to tell me something? We met for lunch. As he was sharing his excitement about the start of his summer program with Athletes in Action, he told me that he believed God had called him to work with gangs. In Los Angeles, California!

> *He was not happy that I wasn't using my newly acquired college degree to go out and get a job and provide for myself.*

I could feel my eyes bulging and my mouth dropping open. I remember saying something like, "OK, Dad and I have been supportive of your working on skid row, but . . . gangs? Are you kidding me?" And he responded by pointing out that I had been just twenty-three years old when I moved to Tijuana. That day my dad, Bud Cooper, must have been rolling over in his grave, laughing hysterically that I was finally experiencing the same emotions he had when I told him I was going to work at the orphanage in Mexico.

In so many ways I can relate to the Bible account of Samuel and his mother, Hannah. I had a hard time getting pregnant, just like Hannah. Scott and I had really wondered if it would ever happen. At just about the time we had made peace that children weren't going to come about in the traditional way for us, I did get pregnant. When Jordan made his decision at eight years old to accept Jesus, I began to see the privilege that God had given Scott and me to raise this little boy to be a man of God.

Hannah turned Samuel over for training to Eli and trusted

her son into his care. She knew that his conception was a miracle, and she committed him to God to be used however he saw fit.

At the lunch with Jordan, I realized that I needed to commit him to God to be used however he saw fit. About Samuel, Hannah had said, "So now I give him to the LORD. For his whole life he will be given over to the LORD" (1 Samuel 1:28).

The epiphany from all this is that we like to say that our children are a gift from God, yet that would imply that we don't have to give them back. I have come to see them as on loan from him. So if a tough oil field worker from West Texas who loved the Lord and raised his children to love the Lord can give his only daughter over to God to be used by him, then anybody can! As a parent, I have also had to learn that lesson myself and turn Jordan over to God to be used by him.

··
Disruptive Questions

1. Read the full account of Hannah and Samuel's story in 1 Samuel 1:1–2:11. What parts of their story can you relate to the most? Why?

2. What are some of the things that you treasure that you would have a hard time giving to the Lord?

3. What is one specific thing that you need to give to the Lord right now? Will you? If yes, how? If no, why not?

the alzheimer's blessing

I n 1 Timothy 5:8, Paul had some pretty strong words as relates to the care of our families. He said, "Anyone who does not provide for their relatives, and especially for their own household, has denied the faith and is worse than an unbeliever."

Cultures all over the world provide for their families, and especially their elderly, in different ways. Even in our American culture we differ on this issue. Some people would never think of putting their parents in a nursing home, so they choose to take on the caregiving themselves. Others believe it is a natural progression for their elderly parents to go to a nursing home, and some people actually believe they need feel no responsibility for their parents at all.

In July 1994, I was walking out the door to catch a plane to a convention, when the phone rang. It was my dad crying and saying he didn't think he could take it much longer. My mother had been diagnosed with Alzheimer's about nine years earlier at the young age of sixty. Dad had cared for her all those years, and he was at the end of his rope.

My dad asked if Scott and I would take her in and care

for her. We both knew that my dad had suffered enough. He had provided for us over the years, and now it was our time to provide for him and care for our relative. We felt that the instruction Paul had given to the church in 1 Timothy 5:8 was for us.

That October, Jordan and I flew back to my childhood home and made the arrangements to bring Mom home with us. I remember asking myself several times that day if I was really prepared to take this on. That flight was a symbolic preview of what was to come. We had one of those routes that stopped two times before landing in San Diego, and turbulence made the flight bumpy the whole way.

One of my first lessons in caring for my mom was that people with Alzheimer's don't care about the "fasten your seat belt" sign that says you cannot get up and move around the cabin. When a person with Alzheimer's needs to go, she will go no matter what!

What I remember most from that day was the shedding of tears and asking myself how I was going to do all that I was doing in the ministry, plus care for my family, and now add my mother with Alzheimer's to the mix.

As I was feeling overwhelmed and a little sorry for myself, I was startled to hear a burst of laughter beside me. I looked over to see Jordan tickling my mom. They were laughing hysterically. It was in that aha moment that I realized I could view this either as a burden or a blessing.

I chose blessing.

It was in that aha moment that I realized I could view this either as a burden or a blessing.

God isn't asking us to care for our relatives because he wants to burden us. He genuinely wants to use these times as teaching moments. God wanted our family to do it because he knew that our time with my mom would be such a blessing and that we would learn life lessons that we couldn't have learned any other way. He was right and we did.

You may be called on to do something similar to what our family did. Are you ready to respond by seeing it as a blessing?

Life-Challenging

DISRUPTION

Your life challenge this month is to read the Bible story of Noah in Genesis 6–9 and make note of the things he did to take care of his family. Then commit to care for a family member this month in a way that shows you love that person. Here are some practical suggestions for how to do that:

- If you live with your family, do one chore a week for a family member.
- If someone in your immediate or extended family is facing a serious illness, commit to being a consistent presence and help for that person.
- If your family is not close by, pick up the phone and call them to encourage them.

Lord, this month I commit to care for a family member in a way that demonstrates my love.

Signature _____ Date _____

on cleaning
bedpans

My pastor friend from San Francisco, the late Bill Miles, said something to me many years ago that had a real impact on me. He said that anyone could go on a hospital visit and pray with the person who is sick, but the true test of character was the ability to clean the person's bedpan.

I think Jesus cleaned some serious "bedpans" during his public ministry. In the Gospels of Matthew, Mark, and Luke we can read the accounts of Jesus healing a man with leprosy, who was not only ravaged by this skin disease but was also an outcast of society. Jesus could have simply prayed with the man and walked away without healing or touching him. But he didn't. It is recorded in Matthew 8:3 that "Jesus reached out his hand and touched the man"—which was unheard of during that day.

Years ago I was asked to serve in the summer program of an urban church because the church was dying and the leaders wanted it to grow. I would venture to say that the members of the church were a bit surprised when the kids we invited into the church from that community weren't exactly the profile they were looking for in growing their church. At some point I realized that we could bring in one million kids and it wouldn't matter—because the ones who were coming didn't smell good, and some even had lice.

I had a very interesting conversation with an elder of that church. He said, "Gayla, you think in order to touch people with God's love, you have to physically touch them. Well, you don't." That was probably the day I realized I was a bedpan cleaner. And I also knew then that my days were numbered at that church.

Jesus got into a heap of trouble with the Pharisees, a group of influential religious leaders, for cleaning bedpans. When he healed a blind man (John 9), the Pharisees investigated the healing because Jesus had performed it on a holy day. It was obviously a no-no, and God forbid that someone needed his bedpan cleaned on that day!

> *I think Jesus cleaned some serious "bedpans"*
> *during his public ministry.*

My saintly husband turned out to be a bedpan cleaner when he not only agreed to take in my mother when she had Alzheimer's but also became committed to her care. It was my hope during her time with us that Scott would not be called on to bathe her. I had a meeting in St. Louis that had me leaving early Monday and returning on Tuesday evening. Before I left that morning, I gave my mother a bath and told Scott that she would be fine until I returned the next day.

As you have probably figured out, something happened

that required Scott to give her a bath. I can remember laughing together later about the events that led up to his bathing her. My complete love and admiration grew for this man who became the ultimate cleaner of bedpans.

Honestly, I'm not a natural cleaner of bedpans. It's just too messy, and I don't like messes. But when your life is disrupted, you commit to doing more than praying for people. You clean their bedpans!

Disruptive Questions

1. What people do you see in our society today that are often treated like modern-day untouchables? Do you think God has called you to do anything about that? If so, what?

2. Do you have a bedpan story? What is it? What did you learn from that experience?

3. Are there people you know personally who need God's love but you have a hard time reaching out to touch them? How can you change that?

who is the servant of all?

You can't be both Mary and Martha at the same time. Either you are Mary, the sister who sat at Jesus' feet and listened while doing nothing, or you are Martha, the sister who was running around like a chicken with her head cut off while doing all the work.

Can you guess which sister I relate to more? Yes, I admit that I've never been a fan of Mary and have always believed that Martha got a bad rap in these verses from Luke 10:38-42:

> As Jesus and his disciples were on their way, he came to a village where a woman named Martha opened her home to him. She had a sister called Mary, who sat at the Lord's feet listening to what he said. But Martha was distracted by all the preparations that had to be made. She came to him and asked, "Lord, don't you care that my sister has left me to do the work by myself? Tell her to help me!"
>
> "Martha, Martha," the Lord answered, "you are worried and upset about many things, but few things are needed—or indeed only one. Mary has chosen

what is better, and it will not be taken away from her."

I get what Jesus was saying and how Martha, just like myself at times, got caught up in trying to be the servant of all. Here's one of my Martha moments.

After seeing the movies *Blindside* and *Invictus*, I began to ask myself the question, "Have I done enough?" In the interest of doing more, Scott and I had the opportunity to volunteer with our church, Solana Beach Presbyterian, when it closed its doors one Sunday morning to send members all over San Diego County to serve. In complete honesty, I loved telling people about the sacrifice Scott and I were making by participating in this project—knowing just how impressed they would be, given how much we already do, of course!

I was able to find a project close to our home, where we could go for three hours to clean a Boys and Girls Club. Those who know me well are aware of what a clean freak I am (read: borderline OCD). Thus, I was happy when I was assigned to clean the kitchen—until I walked into the kitchen alone. No one else wanted to be assigned that project!

After seeing the movies Blindside *and* Invictus, *I began to ask myself the question, "Have I done enough?"*

The first thought going through my mind was how much better I could organize that kitchen. While cleaning the walls where food had landed after missing the trash can, I was thinking how I never would have let that happen under my watch.

I'm not done. Three other volunteers were spending their time organizing all the board games. They spent three hours counting Monopoly money! That takes three people!? And the more they laughed and talked, the more frustrated I became.

Because I was by myself in that dirty kitchen doing *real* volunteer work.

At some point I began envisioning an awards ceremony at the end of our project, where I was crowned the servant of all!

I know what you are thinking, and you're right. My ramblings sounded like Martha, who wanted Mary to help out a little when Jesus visited. So my apologies to those three women who organized the board games. They came to serve that day with joyful hearts and made me ask myself, "Who's the servant of all?"

Let's be honest—every one of us sometimes makes the mistake Martha and I made. All we need to do is look at Philippians 2:5-8 as a reminder of the supreme example of the one who was really the servant of all.

····························
Disruptive Questions

1. Who do you identify more with in Luke 10:38-42, Mary or Martha? Why? Are there specific memories that you have concerning a Mary or Martha moment?

2. Have you ever gotten so busy *serving* God that you *forgot about* God? What happened?

3. Being honest, have you ever thought God was pretty fortunate to have you on his team? What did you do to change your attitude?

my father's business

I have always loved the story of Jesus at the temple when he was twelve years old. In the Luke 2:41-52 account, his parents, Joseph and Mary, had taken him with them to the Feast of the Passover in Jerusalem. While they were returning home, they realized that Jesus was not with them.

As we read this story, we find out that Jesus had a really good reason for staying behind. I love this story because when I was twelve, I would have loved hanging out with someone who had the courage to upset his parents for something he knew to be right.

Of course, Mary was upset and wondered why Jesus would treat them that way. This would be equivalent to a group leader thinking he had all his students when they left Mexico, only to find that they had left someone behind. Not like that has ever happened, right?

Jesus gave an answer that even Scripture says his parents didn't understand. He asked them two questions: "Why were you searching for me?" and "Didn't you know I had to be in my Father's house?" (v. 49).

I am not sure whether that answer would pacify any parent;

but at the end of this account, it does say that Jesus returned home to Nazareth and was obedient to them. His mother treasured all these things in her heart and watched him find favor with God and men.

At an early age Jesus seemed to grasp something that it takes most of us our whole lives to get. He understood that his life was to be "about my Father's business" (*KJV*). In how Jesus lived, we see the example he set for us to also be about our Father's business.

A former member of our staff, Chelsea Oldroyd Enderle, shared a story with me upon her return from serving in Puerto Peñasco. She and a couple of other staff members were at the beach on their time off and met a man who had a prosthetic leg and lived in an abandoned building. He told the group how cold it got at night.

> *At an early age Jesus seemed to grasp something that it takes most of us our whole lives to get.*

After leaving the beach, Chelsea couldn't stop thinking about the man and felt that God was telling her to get him a blanket. She only slightly remembered what the man had said about where he worked, and she wasn't even sure about his name. Two things needed to happen: Chelsea needed a blanket and needed to find the man.

Both things happened without any orchestration on her part.

A group donated blankets to give to families. So now she

had the blanket. As she and another staff member, Jonathan, prayed and looked for the man high and low, God parted the Red Sea of a crowded street in Puerto Peñasco, and out of nowhere the man appeared.

Chelsea was there to help oversee seven work sites. But because she was about her Father's business, she also gave warmth to a cold and homeless man.

When we commit ourselves to being about our Father's business, God does the incredible.

Disruptive Questions

1. Put yourself in the shoes of Mary and Joseph when they realized that their child was missing. What emotions would you have been experiencing?

2. Jesus believed that he was going about his Father's business when he was in the temple talking about God. What does it look like for you to be about your Father's business in your daily life now?

3. List some other practical ways that you could be about your Father's business.

keep warm and well fed

An African proverb says, "An empty stomach has no ears to hear with." This reminds me of a story shared by one of my former students when I was teaching a class on urban ministry.

At the time, we were having a lively discussion about evangelism and social action. My student's family worked as missionaries in a country where the Communists were causing people to flee that country and cross over into a neighboring land. Their plight included a lack of food and water. The good news was that missionaries were waiting for these people, when they crossed from one country into the other, with the resources to meet their basic needs. The student pointed out that when those refugees arrived, they were starving and dying of thirst. They needed a cup of cold water in Jesus' name before they could hear someone preaching.

First John 3:17, 18 puts it like this: "If anyone has material possessions and sees a brother or sister in need but has no pity on them, how can the love of God be in that person? Dear children, let us not love with words or speech but with actions and in truth." And James asks, "If one of you says to them, 'Go in peace; keep warm and well fed,' but does nothing about their physical needs, what good is it?" (James 2:16).

When people go on short-term mission trips, one of the greatest impacts on them is how differently they view their material possessions after the trip. Steve Horrex came on one of those trips. That's when he told my husband, "Even though I love what you are doing, I could never do it!"

How often have people told God that they couldn't or wouldn't do something—only to find themselves doing that exact thing? Seven months after Steve made that pronouncement to Scott, he was driving from his home in Canada to be a missionary in Mexico. In order to do that, he had to sell most of his material possessions. Steve embodies the true spirit of both of those Scripture passages quoted above. After going on a short-term trip, his worldview was altered. That led him to make the commitment to being a missionary. Thirty years later he is still doing that thing he said he could never do!

> *How often have people told God that they couldn't or wouldn't do something—only to find themselves doing that exact thing?*

The work that Amor Ministries does in building homes in the Tijuana dump originated with Steve. He designed our first house, and these are still the house plans we use in Mexico. He has even created new designs for the houses that are being built in South Africa and on the San Carlos Apache Reservation near Globe, Arizona.

Steve was never going to be an evangelist in the traditional sense. I probably should not say *never*, because our God can do the impossible. It's just that I don't imagine you'll ever find Steve preaching in a pulpit. But I can't think of anyone who has done more to keep people warm and well fed than Steve Horrex. No matter what Steve does, he always leads people to Jesus.

May you follow his example.

Life-Challenging

DISRUPTION

Your life challenge this month is to research how many people in the world live without clean water and the difference that clean water would make to them. Then commit to give up your favorite drink for this month and donate the money saved to a clean water program. Here are some practical suggestions for how to do this:

- Give up soda or juice and drink water instead.
- If you order lattes or other fancy coffee drinks, switch to make-your-own coffee at home for the month.
- You can find clean water programs at www.armor.org/give/projecthope and www.givecleanwater.org. These programs teach the families how to clean their water!

Lord, this month I commit to giving up my favorite drink in order to save money and donate to a clean water program.

Signature _____   Date _____

hard is better

John F. Kennedy said, "We choose to go to the moon in this decade and do the other things, not because they are easy, but because they are hard, because that goal will serve to organize and measure the best of our energies and skills, because that challenge is one that we are willing to accept, one we are unwilling to postpone, and one which we intend to win, and the others, too."[34]

That quote from President Kennedy was given in a speech he delivered at Rice Stadium on September 12, 1962. It concerned why the United States was going to the moon. It hearkens back to a time when choosing "the road less traveled" was expected if you wanted to make your mark on the world.

That's why the Amor philosophy is about coming on a trip where, for one week of your life, you live, eat, and serve close to the experience of those you are working alongside. During the time our participants spend on the field, we want them to enter into the culture of those whom they are serving. It is our desire that they return home with a better understanding of the challenges faced by those living in poverty and then commit to do something about it.

In the book *Lives Built on Hope*, Amor staff member Howard Major frames it like this:

We do not allow the use of power tools in this Ministry. We mix concrete and stucco by hand. We do not use cement mixers, generators, circular saws, or nail guns. . . . Our philosophy is to use hand tools with inexpensive, indigenous materials to build a modest home that can be maintained and improved after we leave. Instead of overpowering our host families, we empower them with examples of what they can do for themselves without big, expensive tools. We also teach basic life skills to those participants who have never before hit a nail or cut a piece of wood.[35]

I like to compare our process to Romans 12:1, which says, "I urge you, brothers and sisters, in view of God's mercy, to offer your bodies as a living sacrifice, holy and pleasing to God—this is your true and proper worship." For those on an Amor trip, mixing concrete by hand for the foundation of the house will be a sacrifice of one's body. Day one of our trips is the toughest—that is, if you don't have to spend your whole first day leveling the site before you pour the slab.

> *Mixing concrete by hand for the foundation of the house will be a sacrifice of one's body.*

Hard is better. As Howard says,

Perhaps we could build bigger, faster, and better; but then, we would forget why we came to serve. You have to spend a week with one of these families—living and working with them in their world to understand how this works. Once, upon the completion and blessing of the home, the new homeowner said, "I appreciate the home and the hard work very much but even more, I am grateful that strangers came to share their lives with me."[36]

When we started building houses, quite a few classmates from Pacific Christian College came with Amor as we served at a Tijuana orphanage. It was the first mission trip for many of them. One of them called after going on that first trip and said that he was going to do something different that summer because the "house-building project was just too hard!" A few others didn't even have the courage to call and tell me; I heard it from other friends and sometimes from their spouses.

If you don't know this already, I hate to be the one to break it to you—sometimes God's work is hard.

God could have made it easy for Jesus. But that didn't happen, and we are the beneficiaries. Hard is better.

Disruptive Questions

1. What is one of the hardest things you've ever had to do? What made it so hard?

2. What is something hard that the Lord asked you to do in direct service to him? Did you do it? If so, how did that help make you stronger?

3. In what specific ways are you willing to give your body as a sacrifice to do his work?

the power of
our words

Walter Hochstader, a German pastor during World War II, wrote, "The Church ought to live of love. Woe to her if she does not do that! Woe to her if by her silence and by all sorts of dubious excuses she becomes jointly guilty of the world's outbursts of hatred! Woe to her if she adopts words and slogans that originate in the sphere of hatred."[37]

You've probably heard the phrase "Sticks and stones may break my bones, but words will never hurt me." It simply isn't true. Words are powerful; and when spoken with anger and in a spirit of meanness, they can leave an indelible print on someone long after a bone would have healed.

One day I was sitting with the pastoral staff and church leaders who were discussing their upcoming trip to Mexico. You can imagine how I felt when one gentleman informed me that there were people in the church who just hated Mexico—and Mexicans! In my most diplomatic voice—and I will admit that I don't really *have* a diplomatic voice—I spoke very softly and told him that, given the words of Jesus to "love our neighbors," hating Mexico and Mexicans is just not an option for Christians.

The anger in some people's voices reveals an attitude that borders on the hatred that Pastor Hochstader spoke of. Jesus said, "The things that come out of a person's mouth come from the heart, and these defile them" (Matthew 15:18). What comes out of our mouths is a true reflection of what is in our hearts. It is disconcerting that demeaning and harsh words are even spoken in the church. There are those who give that as their reason for not attending church. They may either have heard these words or personally have borne the brunt of the words themselves. The good news is that there are many people who are part of the church because someone was encouraging and spoke kindly to them.

In the book of Proverbs, references to our use of words, lips, mouths, and tongues appear about 150 times in the 31 chapters. Why? Because our tongues are moving all day long, and they do tell the story of what is going on in our hearts. Unfortunately, what we say is not always in harmony with the holiness of God. I believe that having problems with our mouths is a spiritual issue we all face—some more than others.

Our tongues are moving all day long, and they do tell the story of what is going on in our hearts.

My challenge to all of us is that we should use words that genuinely reflect Christ's nature and his character of love. In our everyday lives and in our homes, when we speak with those who hold views different from ours, let us remember the power of our words. And may those of us in the church be unified in civility toward one another in spite of these differences. It is my sincere prayer that those who are marginalized in our world will hear and see the love of God as evidenced in the power of our words and deeds!

"May these words of my mouth and this meditation of my heart be pleasing in your sight, LORD, my Rock and my Redeemer" (Psalm 19:14).

Disruptive Questions

1. Read Proverbs 13:3 and 16:24. What do these verses say about the power of our lips and tongues to bless or to curse?

2. Was there ever a time in your life when someone's words impacted you in a negative way . . . and those words still have an effect on you to this day? What happened?

3. Have you ever spoken some words that you would like to take back? What did you learn from the situation? Were you able to go back and right your wrong? What happened?

living as the church

Christians all over the world prepare their hearts and homes each Easter to celebrate the resurrection of the Lord Jesus Christ. The story of the empty tomb is powerful, and the early church was established on this foundation: Jesus Christ, crucified and raised to life.

Because my parents raised my brothers and me in the church, I have a deep love and affection for it. I stand in awe of the men and women who sacrificed their lives so that the church could be birthed.

As I grew up, the church was a place of acceptance for me. A place where a chubby, little eight-year-old girl wearing cat eyeglasses could flourish. I wanted to be a missionary so I could tell others how great it was to follow Jesus and that being in the church was the best part of my life. I thought there was nothing better than being a Whirlybird or Jet Cadet for Jesus in our children's program. You may have no idea what I'm talking about. The Whirlybird and Jet Cadet programs were different age levels of curriculum that our Sunday school teacher used to teach us about following Jesus.

At a church I visited recently, the theme of the service

concerned the staggering statistics of young people leaving the church or showing no interest at all. The *Christian Post* cited that a study from the Barna group "found that nearly three out of every five young Christians (59 percent) disconnect from church life, either permanently or for a long period of time after the age of 15."[38]

> *Because my parents raised my brothers and me in the church, I have a deep love and affection for it.*

What is the mission of the church? Jesus seemed to understand that leaving the throne of God, going to the cross, rising from the dead, and laying the foundation for the establishment of the church was his mission and purpose. That's plenty! But he did even more. Throughout his public ministry Jesus gave us a road map to follow. I wonder what the church would look like if we followed his map. At its core, the gospel message is really about Jesus' nature and character.

Let's look at Jesus' character for a moment. He cared for the poor and marginalized. He showed compassion toward tax collectors as well as prostitutes. He touched people who had leprosy. Some of his disciples were lowly fishermen. And he intentionally went through Samaria and spoke with the woman at the well (both Samaria and the woman were things he had been taught to avoid). Jesus despised exploitation, which was why he overturned the tables of the money changers.

Jesus told us to love our neighbors, and he defined our neighbor as anyone in need. And in Matthew 25 he compelled us to love "the least of these," saying that whatever we do for them, we are doing for him.

I worked in Mexico with a church where their pastor was preaching a sermon series entitled "It's not what you believe, but how you live." The series was teaching that as Christians we sometimes have different beliefs from each other and yet we can all live out the character of Jesus. What is that? Philippians 2:5-7 challenges us: "In your relationships with one another, have the same mindset as Christ Jesus: Who, being in very nature God, did not consider equality with God something to be used to his own advantage; rather, he made himself nothing by taking the very nature of a servant."

More than any time of the year, during spring I get to see thousands of people live out their faith in different ways as they come to one of our locations and work alongside a needy family to build a home. When they do so, they are living out Jesus' desires, and they are being the church.

Disruptive Questions

1. Do you have some good memories of the church while you were growing up? If so, what are some of them?

2. What are some things you love about the church? What are some things that could be improved on in the church? What part could you play in this improvement, instead of just complaining?

3. If you are part of the body of Christ, the church, what are some specific things you can you do to help the church fulfill its mission?

be a first responder

An angel of the Lord appeared to Philip, one of Jesus' disciples, and told him to go down the desert road from Jerusalem to Gaza. On his way he came upon an Ethiopian who was sitting in his chariot on the side of the road, reading from the book of Isaiah.

This was no chance encounter. In the Acts 8:26-40 account, we find Philip asking the Ethiopian if he understood what he was reading. The man said he didn't, so Philip joined him in the chariot and shared with him the gospel of Jesus.

Here's the best part of the story. As the chariot was moving along that desert road with the Ethiopian and Philip on board, it came to a body of water. Because of what the man had just heard, he asked that the chariot be pulled over so he could be baptized right then and there! He didn't ask to go home so he could think about what he had heard—he responded immediately.

One of America's most respected correspondents, Jim Wooten, is the author of the book *We Are All the Same*, the story of a young South African boy whom Nelson Mandela called "an icon of the struggle for life."[39] Nkosi Johnson's life was too short, and yet the impact of his twelve years was so well known that his obituary made the front page of newspapers all over the world in 2001.

Originally given only a few years to live, as a result of being infected with the HIV virus in his mother's womb, this little Zulu boy defied the odds; and by the time he was eight years old, he had lived longer than any child born with HIV in all of Africa.

I never had the privilege of meeting Nkosi Johnson. But I have met the woman from that book who believed she had to respond to the three-year-old boy who had been courageously brought to her AIDS hospice by his mother Daphne. Gail Johnson took Nkosi in and raised him as her own—and together they confronted HIV/AIDS in South Africa.

Recently, I found a brochure in my files that was over twenty years old. It concerned a ministry committed to those affected by AIDS. This group of Christians confronted the church with what they believed to be a failure in reaching out to those who were living with HIV/AIDS, because of fear, ignorance, and critical judgment.

> *Gail Johnson took Nkosi in and raised him as her own— and together they confronted HIV/AIDS in South Africa.*

This is bigger than just the AIDS issue. It's any issue that we Christians don't know how to deal with. In 1988, Tony Campolo wrote a book about this very thing. It was called *20 Hot Potatoes Christians Are Afraid to Touch*. In the book he discussed abortion, homosexuality, and women in leadership—to name a few of those hot potatoes. They are issues that we are still dealing with today; and to me, no Christian leader has addressed them better than Dr. Campolo.

In the summer of 2012, I joined women from five different countries to visit Nkosi's Haven in South Africa. We met a mother who had traveled from Zimbabwe to bring her son to be cared for at this facility. She spoke of how warm her heart was to see so many women holding and kissing the children.

You could tell that this mother was touched by the women helping to tear down the stigma associated with AIDS by the love that was shown that day to the moms and their babies. We've a ways to go in dealing with this issue, but I believe we have come a long way! It was evident that day at Nkosi's Haven.

Many years ago, the Ethiopian on the side of the road was compelled to respond once he heard the gospel of Jesus. Gail Johnson responded by changing the face of HIV/AIDS on the continent of Africa. And as followers of Jesus, we must respond to the needs that we see around us.

Life-Challenging

DISRUPTION

Your life challenge this month is to think about these three questions:

1. Why does it sometimes seem like the church takes so long to respond to an issue that Jesus would (and did) respond to immediately? Research leprosy (a couple of

sources are http://www.cdc.gov/nczved/divisions/dfbmd/ diseases/hansens_disease/technical.html and http://www.e-summit.org/conference/Jesus-and-Justice.html). Then read Matthew 8:1-4 to see how Jesus responded to people with leprosy.

2. Why do we often have to wait for an issue like AIDS to affect us personally before we respond?

3. What would motivate you personally to respond to these kinds of needs around you, both locally and globally?

Commit to be a person who follows the example of Jesus by responding quickly. Here are some suggestions to help you do that:

- Ask yourself what your most distasteful or feared issue is; then go volunteer to help those who are affected.
- Think about something that is happening in our culture that you believe the church should respond to. Be bold by stepping out and educating yourself on that issue, and then do something tangible and find a way to support the cause. Finally, commit to raising awareness in those around you.
- Read about one big issue at www.stopthetraffik.org.

Lord, this month I commit to be a first responder.

Signature _____ Date _____

the great commission

hen Jesus came to them and said, 'All authority in heaven and on earth has been given to me. Therefore go and make disciples of all nations, baptizing them in the name of the Father and of the Son and of the Holy Spirit, and teaching them to obey everything I have commanded you. And surely I am with you always, to the very end of the age" (Matthew 28:18-20).

Have you ever seen those rainbow-colored beanies with the propeller that spins on the top? If you have, you can envision me as a nine-year-old, proudly wearing one each week for our Whirlybird program at my church. At that program my friends and I were asked by the teacher to memorize these verses from Matthew. I did that because I knew there would be a sweet reward for doing so!

Every time I memorized Scripture verses, I tried my best to live them out. When I was in the third grade, my friend and I came up with an idea for how we both could live out the Matthew 28 verses. In my own words, I wrote the Christmas story, and my friend drew a picture of what it looked like. Then we went door to door in our neighborhood, knocking and asking each family if I could read the story I had written, while my friend held up her picture. Pretty sweet, huh?

Since it was the holiday season, we were bestowed with Christmas treats of fudge, divinity, and sugar cookies. This was probably the reason that our motives began to shift somewhere around the fifth house.

A few years later, Matthew 28:18-20 provided the motivation for me to invite my next-door neighbors to church. This Mexican family consisted of the parents and two children. The children were about my age, and we had become close friends. I asked the family if they would like to join us one Sunday at church. The family accepted and became more than neighbors as we all started going to church together each week.

I have often wondered if that first experience of my reaching out to someone in this way was an indicator that God was developing in me a heart for the Mexican culture. At an early age I understood that the Great Commission was a command to reach beyond our own culture and share the love of Jesus with those who represented "all nations."

One of my heroes is someone I never had the privilege of meeting. But I have read the story of Chet Bitterman's commitment to living out the Great Commission. These verses in Matthew steered him to become a linguist with Wycliffe Bible Translators.

At an early age I understood that the Great Commission was a command to reach beyond our own culture and share the love of Jesus with those who represented "all nations."

Chet felt that the best way for him to fulfill the Great Commission was to go to Colombia so he could translate the Bible for a tribal group who did not have God's Word in their language. Unfortunately, Chet was murdered in Bogotá, Columbia, before he was able to fulfill his goal. M-19 guerrillas, who were looking for the director of the Summer Institute of Linguistics, kidnapped Bitterman instead.

Two years before his death, Bitterman had written this in his journal: "The situation in Nicaragua is getting worse. If Nicaragua falls, I guess the rest of Central America will too. Maybe this is just some kind of self-inflicted Martyr complex, but I find this recurring thought that perhaps God will call me to be martyred in His service in Colombia. I am willing."[40] Chet Bitterman was willing to live and die for the Great Commission.

Disruptive Questions

1. Can you recall an experience in which you attempted to share Jesus' love with someone when you were young? Or did someone else share the message of Jesus with you first? What happened?

2. How important is it to you to share your faith today? What are your favorite ways to do so?

3. What would you be willing to die for?

when you feel like running

once found myself nose to nose with a mother who was a member of one of the most violent gangs in Hawaiian Gardens, California. If I had blinked she would have punched me. I had reported to social services that her child had come to our summer program with iron burns on his legs. I stood like the Queen's guard outside Buckingham Palace as this woman threatened my life. My body didn't budge since I felt like my life was on the line, but in my heart I wanted to cut and run.

In 1 Kings 19 we learn that the prophet Elijah had a moment when he cut and ran. After God had used him to defeat the prophets of Baal (1 Kings 18), Queen Jezebel retaliated by threatening Elijah's life. As a result I can imagine that he might have felt depressed, abandoned, and most likely, angry with God. He had done what God had told him to do, and yet Elijah felt let down by God. I know I have in those situations. So he ran to the desert where he wanted to die.

When our lives are disrupted, we are compelled to make ourselves available to God. But not every one of those situations is going to be a feel-good story. Some of them are going to be like what Elijah encountered with Jezebel—and what I encountered in Hawaiian Gardens. Our natural instinct might be to cut and run.

Elijah made some bad decisions along the way. James 5:17 says, "Elijah was a human being, even as we are." God still chose to work through Elijah in spite of himself, and he will work through us even after we have cut and run.

Elijah is known as God's most dramatic, forceful prophet. He stopped the rain, he went toe to toe with a king, caused fire to rain down from Heaven, ordered the execution of hundreds of false prophets, and accurately predicted the day when a three-year drought would end. And if that wasn't enough, Elijah restored a dead child to his mother!

What seemed like a decision to be a lone ranger may have caused him to feel abandoned and isolated. But through it all Elijah responded to the greatest miracle of all. He was able to know God intimately because God makes himself available to us—not always in the shouts, but more frequently in the persistent whispers.

Here's how it went down with Elijah:

> The LORD said, "Go out and stand on the mountain in the presence of the LORD, for the LORD is about to pass by."
>
> Then a great and powerful wind tore the mountains apart and shattered the rocks before the LORD, but the LORD was not in the wind. After the wind there was an earthquake, but the LORD was not in the earthquake. After the earthquake came a fire, but the LORD was not in the fire. And after the fire came a gentle whisper (1 Kings 19:11, 12).

God understands our desire to cut and run. But he knows that if we listen to his gentle whisper on a daily basis, then we can overcome fear and failure. From the Elijah account we learn that even when facing an angry gang member, we are never alone. God is always there. No need to cut and run—he's got your back.

....
Disruptive Questions

1. Have you ever felt like Elijah, abandoned by God, even though you had done what God asked of you? What happened? How did you resolve the situation?

2. Have you ever cut and run? If so, how did you make your way back to God?

3. The next time you feel like running, what can you hold on to that will help you stand your ground? Memorize Psalm 23 and John 16:33 for future reference.

who's afeared?

hate snakes. I'm OK with bugs, spiders, and even mice—but definitely not snakes. If a snake appears on a TV show, I turn the channel immediately. Growing up in West Texas where they catch rattlesnakes and fry them up . . . creeps me out just writing about it! I have a phobia that probably wasn't helped by being told one night when I was in my teens to be still, as I had stepped into the coil of a rattlesnake. The plan was for my best friend's dad to kill the snake and then help me remove my foot from the coil.

I did not follow that plan. The story goes that as soon as I heard the word *rattlesnake*, I ran. They said that the adrenaline alone must have been the reason they found me two miles down the road from their house!

Fears about those things that could potentially harm us are natural, and we should have a healthy respect for them. And yet I don't believe that God ever meant for us to live in the kind of fear where our lives become paralyzed and we can miss out on doing what God has called us to do.

In the 1920s, Germany faced major issues of unemployment and inflation. Hitler came along and offered security against those issues, and the people—giving in to their fears—ended up doing terrible things.

If fear ruled my life, then:

- I never would have left my small town.
- I never would have gone to Mexico to live.
- I never would have started Amor Ministries.
- I never would have moved my family into the inner city.
- I would have packed it in on many occasions over the years when it got tough.
- I would have said no to God every time he asked me to step out in faith and trust him.

That list could go on and on. So what do you fear? Cultivating a mission-focused life means you will probably be asked to serve people in places where you never thought you would go. It seems as though God likes to put us in situations that challenge our worldview. He wants us to be uncomfortable, and that's a good thing. But when we don't feel in control of our destiny, fears can creep in.

In his book *In a Pit with a Lion on a Snowy Day*, Mark Batterson has this to say: "Too often our prayers revolve around asking God to reduce the odds in our lives. We want everything in our favor. But maybe God wants to stack the odds against us so we can experience a miracle of divine proportions. Maybe faith is trusting God no matter how impossible the odds are. Maybe our impossible situations are opportunities to experience a new dimension of God's glory."[41]

Wendy Johnson joined our staff with a plan to stay long enough to get us organized. I think she said two years tops. Wendy definitely didn't see herself as a missionary. Actually, she was part of a group of students at Pacific Christian College who made fun of those students who went down to Mexico each weekend with Amor. When she thought about working at Amor, she was afraid of what God would ask her to change in her life. However, over an almost nineteen-year period on our staff, she not only got us organized, but she took on the heart of a missionary. And boy, am I grateful!

Our fears are not always based on the potential of encountering a physical danger—though in the Bible we have numerous examples where that was the case. Shadrach, Meshach, and Abednego were in the fiery furnace. Daniel was in the lions' den, Paul and Silas in a jail cell. Do I think they were afraid? Absolutely! But all those people put their fears aside and placed their lives on the line for God.

> *Cultivating a mission-focused life means you will probably be asked to serve people in places that you never thought you would go.*

What we often fear most is being asked to be with those who are different from us. Or that we just might have to sacrifice material rewards. Maybe it's a fear of having to change our dreams to the ones that God has for us.

What should we fear? For me—and snakes aside—it would be *not* living the abundant life God has for me, not being able to abandon all that is safe to live a carelessly passionate life. What is it for you?

Disruptive Questions

1. What are your top five fears?

2. What is the one fear that you don't think God would be able to help you overcome? Why?

3. Challenge yourself to take on one of those five fears and ask God to help you overcome it. Read Romans 8:31-39. Then face that fear!

counting the cost

I f you grew up in the church like I did and you are close to my age, then you probably remember the flannel board your Sunday school teacher used to teach each week's Bible story. I recall my teacher putting up the picture of Jesus standing at the door and knocking. I loved when it was explained to me that the door was my heart and that Jesus wanted to come into my heart. The first time I heard that may have been the moment when I first fell in love with Jesus.

Falling in love with Jesus comes with a cost. Luke 9:23 puts it this way: "Then [Jesus] said to them all: 'Whoever wants to be my disciple must deny themselves and take up their cross daily and follow me.'"

My friend Matt Summerfield did that when he left a lucrative position with T-Mobile and took the position of executive director of Urban Saints, UK. It's what Mark Ritchie, a passionate Scotsman who travels the world communicating the message of the cross, did when he withstood the bullying of lads who were making fun of his Christian faith.

Both stories have something in common. Because of Matt's

and Mark's willingness to take up their crosses and follow Jesus, many lives have been changed.

For Matt, it means that more than forty-five thousand youth and children participate each week in an Urban Saints group. In a recent conversation Matt told my husband and me that he has a goal of reaching two million kids over the next ten years. He walked away from making millions of dollars for his company in order to reach millions of souls for the *real* Jesus, not to be confused with flannel board Jesus.

Falling in love with Jesus comes with a cost.

Mark's best friend (or mate, as he would say) was moved to accept Christ after witnessing Mark's humiliation taking place at the hand of some bullies. When I heard him tell this story, I was touched by the fact that it was what Mark was willing to go through on behalf of Jesus that led this lad to Christ. Just last August, Mark set out on a "Cross Britain" seventy-day mission, in which he walked seven hundred miles of Great Britain while carrying a cross and hosting thirty evangelistic events along the route—with the aim of reaching over seven thousand people with the message of the cross. Concerning the cross of Jesus, Mark says, "Some people will accept it, some will reject it, but no one will ignore it. This is what God has put in my heart to do—to put the Cross in front of Britain."[42]

When you read the account of Queen Esther in the Old Testament book named after her, you learn about the price she was willing to pay on behalf of the Jewish people. The short story is that Esther was an orphan raised by her cousin Mordecai. The Persian King Xerxes married her because of her great beauty.

King Xerxes bestowed on one of his most prominent princes, Haman, the honor of having people bow down to him when he rode his horse through the streets. Mordecai refused to bow down to anyone but God, and that infuriated Haman. His plan to wipe out Mordecai and the entire Jewish population in the Persian Empire would have happened, had Esther not interceded.

By putting their lives at risk, Esther and Mordecai denied themselves in order to "pick up their crosses." With everything on the line, they stood up to a king and a prince because of their unwillingness to bow before anyone other than God.

The stories of Matt, Mark, and Esther all have something in common. In order to follow your Lord, you *will* have to give something up. Following him comes with a cost.

Life-Challenging

DISRUPTION

Your life challenge for this month focuses on Esther and her willingness to put her life on the line for her people. Read the book of Esther as preparation to do something for God that will come at a cost. Here are some suggestions to help you do this:

- If you have trouble praying aloud, the next time you are in a group and have the opportunity, take the risk and pray out loud.

- Take the risk and share your testimony or story with those who may not know about the Jesus who lives in you.
- Share with others the story of a time when you made a sacrifice. Be specific about what it cost you.
- Take the equivalent of one day's vacation money (or whatever would be a big financial sacrifice for you) and use it to do something for someone in your neighborhood, just out of love.

Lord, this month I commit to take
a risk and let my faith be known.

Signature _____ Date _____

a macedonian call

t is possible for us to be moving in one direction while God wants us to go in a different direction. Acts 16:6-10 says,

> Paul and his companions traveled throughout the region of Phrygia and Galatia, having been kept by the Holy Spirit from preaching the word in the province of Asia. When they came to the border of Mysia, they tried to enter Bithynia, but the Spirit of Jesus would not allow them to. So they passed by Mysia and went down to Troas. During the night Paul had a vision of a man of Macedonia standing and begging him, "Come over to Macedonia and help us."
>
> After Paul had seen the vision, we got ready at once to leave for Macedonia, concluding that God had called us to preach the gospel to them.

Paul's obedience to what is known as the Macedonian Call resulted in what is believed to be the first time the gospel was preached in Europe. This occurred because Paul had trusted the Holy Spirit with his travel plans.

Patti Piper and her husband, Dave, were actively involved in mission work—leading a group from their church in Tucson, Arizona, to Puerto Peñasco. Because of their proximity to the work, they were able to visit throughout the year and build strong ties with pastors and families in Mexico. Unbeknownst to Patti, that season in her life was coming to an end; God was going to be taking her in a different direction.

Two years before her final trip to Puerto Peñasco, God started speaking to Patti about Bunco games. Yes, you heard me—Bunco games. As she looks back it was obvious that God knew her time in Mexico was coming to an end and that he was preparing her to serve in a different way. In her heart she was hearing God say that there was a reason for this, to let it happen, and to "just trust me and go with it."

Of course Patti wanted to know where the spiritual application was going to be in all this. Was God actually asking her to go from serving alongside those in physical poverty to playing Bunco?

Was God actually asking her to go from serving alongside those in physical poverty to playing Bunco?

As God began to move Patti away from Mexico, he gave her a heightened sense of loving and listening to people. The question "Do they matter?" was answered with an overwhelming yes. It was about investing in the lives of those who were affected by a different kind of poverty: the poverty of disconnection.

Patti started to form "Bunco Babe" small groups with a few goals in mind:

- to create a place for laughter and fun
- to provide community
- to reach out to those who didn't have a church home
- to just play Bunco!

Patti says all those things are happening at different levels in each group and that God is working in the simple game of Bunco. For instance, one woman joined a Bunco Babe small group just before her husband left her. She felt isolated and abandoned. But she was able to share her feelings of loneliness and hurt with her Bunco Babes. They were there to love her, cry with her, pray with her—and even help her move when she needed to. She says that this "family" of women helped her find comfort and community.

When Patti hears stories like this, she knows that God wants to help people dealing with the poverty of disconnection just as he wants to meet the needs of those living in physical poverty. And when God changed Patti's direction, he was planning to use her in ways she never imagined!

Disruptive Questions

1. How would you react to God if he redirected your life from something you love to something that doesn't make any sense to you at all? How easy or hard would it be for you to adjust your dreams and plans?

2. What kind of trust in God is required to let him "mess with" the life you have planned? How can you develop that kind of trust in a greater way?

3. What are you willing to give up in order to respond to a "Macedonian Call"?

why me, lord?

The letter was sitting in my box in the main office of the church where I serve," said Becky Ahlberg, executive director of My Safe Harbor in Anaheim, California. She wondered what was going on, because the letter had already been opened. It was a short note from a heroin addict who had been arrested for selling and was now in the county jail, on her way to prison.

The addict's children were living with her mother in a house right across the street from the church. All she wanted was for someone from the church to go and check on her girls, as she was worried about them.

Becky admits that she is ashamed that her first thought was, *Great. How did this end up in my box?* But as the family life minister at the time, she knew it really did fall under her area of responsibility.

Realizing that the woman probably wouldn't write again, Becky dropped her a short note and told her that she would be happy to check on her girls. She committed to pray for the woman and asked her to write again. The question that haunts Becky even to this day is, "What if I hadn't answered that letter?"

This reminds me of Moses in Exodus 4:13, when he said to

God, "Pardon your servant, Lord. Please send someone else." God had asked Moses to lead the Israelites out of Egypt, and Moses was asking, "Why me, Lord?"—just as my friend Becky had.

Let's be honest. Most of us have asked that question at one time or another. So often we lack confidence, just like Moses did. He didn't believe the Israelites would listen to him. That is why he put forth his brother Aaron as a better candidate for talking to the people. Moses was afraid no one would believe that the Lord had appeared to him, so God gave him miraculous signs of proof.

> The question that haunts Becky even to this day is, "What if I hadn't answered that letter?"

Another reason we ask the "Why me, Lord?" question is because we don't want to be bothered. It is so easy to be frustrated with "those needy people" who can take up so much of our time. Sometimes we are so busy "serving God" that we can't hear him whisper in our ear concerning a need that he wants us to meet. He reminds us in Exodus 4 that he will prepare us when he asks us to go and serve. "The LORD said to [Moses], 'Who gave human beings their mouths? Who makes them deaf or mute? Who gives them sight or makes them blind? Is it not I, the LORD?'" (v. 11).

Moses did lead the children of Israel out of Egypt and eventually got them to the promised land. Becky began a correspondence with the woman, and twelve years later she and her whole family had become members of the church. The woman is now a member of the church staff and Becky, a music major, now leads a ministry called My Safe Harbor that "empowers single mothers with new resources, relationships, and responsibilities."

Both Moses and Becky were taken out of their comfort zones. Concerning her ministry, Becky has said it is "the hardest work I've ever done—with long days, lots of doubt, and wondering what to do next. And yet I've never been involved in anything that was more consistently confirmed by God's blessing and leading."

Sometimes when you do the hardest thing you think you will ever do, God uses it to bless you and those you have served!

Just ask Becky. Just ask Moses.

Disruptive Questions

1. What need has been brought to your attention . . . that you have deliberately ignored?

2. Is meeting that need so out of your comfort zone that you are willing to tell God no? Why or why not?

3. What attitudes might you need to adjust so that you can ask God *not* "Why me, Lord?" but "What would you have me do, Lord?"

great disrupters

As I made my way through the gymnasium, I had one thing on my mind. It was report card night at the high school, and I was going to find out how Jordan was doing in one of his classes. The teacher hadn't returned any of the papers the students had turned in that semester, and none of us parents of this class had any idea what our children's grades were. And that was not acceptable.

It was finally my turn to meet with the teacher, and boy, was I ready! Only to find out the one thing that I didn't think I would hear on report card night. The teacher still didn't have the grades. Let's just say I was not pleased.

The next day Jordan came home after school and relayed to me a conversation he'd had with the teacher, who said, "Your mother got all up in my face!" I would say that I *disrupted* Jordan's teacher on that report card night.

We all need disrupters in our lives. Disrupters are people who often say things to us that we don't want to hear. For example, the prophet Nathan caused a little bit of a disruption in King David's life. Being sent by God, Nathan related this story to David that is recorded in 2 Samuel 12:1-4:

There were two men in a certain town, one rich and

the other poor. The rich man had a very large number of sheep and cattle, but the poor man had nothing except one little ewe lamb he had bought. He raised it, and it grew up with him and his children. It shared his food, drank from his cup and even slept in his arms. It was like a daughter to him.

Now a traveler came to the rich man, but the rich man refrained from taking one of his sheep or cattle to prepare a meal for the traveler who had come to him. Instead, he took the ewe lamb that belonged to the poor man and prepared it for the one who had come to him.

When the king heard this story, he was furious with the man, believing that he deserved death. Nathan was using the story to point out to David how he had acted in the same way when he took another man's wife—and made matters worse by having that man killed.

We all need disrupters in our lives. Disrupters are people who often say things to us that we don't want to hear.

David was disrupted. You can see by reading Psalm 51 how great his disruption was.

The first disrupter in my life was Don Hinkle. He was the minister at my home church when I made the commitment to be a missionary.

Even though I made a promise at the age of nine to be a

missionary, between nine and nineteen I didn't think much about that commitment.

As only God can orchestrate, Don had moved from our church and was serving at the Christian church in the city where I attended college. He called me into his office one day and asked about that promise I had made as a young girl to serve God as a missionary. I basically said I didn't think he should hold me to that promise because I had been too young to know what I was doing.

Well, you know how that conversation turned out. Almost forty years later I am the result of a colossal disruption on the part of the minister who baptized me and held me accountable to that promise I made on a summer night in the Guadalupe Mountains of West Texas and Eastern New Mexico.

It is my deepest desire that in this journey of life, God will continue to send his disrupters my way! And I wish for you the same.

Disruptive Questions

1. What does it mean to be a disrupter of others in a spiritual sense?

2. What people has God used as disrupters in your life? How did they disrupt you?

3. Have you ever been a disrupter for someone else? What happened? Do you feel God calling you to the "ministry of disruption" for someone in your life presently? How so?

something different

The apostle Paul's life turned out much different than he had planned. He had a name change during his life and went from being a persecutor of Christians to becoming one of them. Those are real paradigm shifts in a lifetime!

As a Roman citizen, Paul (earlier known as Saul), was well educated in both Hebrew and Greek and was considered extremely influential in the Jewish community. I bet he was pretty content with his life as a Pharisee and all the benefits that went with that position (see Philippians 3:4-6). But God had something different in mind for him.

You can read the account of Paul's conversion to Christianity in Acts 9:1-19. Here's the gist of that day on the road to Damascus when Saul of Tarsus was disrupted. His life would never be the same again.

As he neared Damascus on his journey, suddenly a light from heaven flashed around him. He fell to the ground and heard a voice say to him, "Saul, Saul, why do you persecute me?"

"Who are you, Lord?" Saul asked.

"I am Jesus, whom you are persecuting," he replied. "Now get up and go into the city, and you will be told what you must do" (vv. 3-6).

When Saul pulled himself up off the ground, he was blind and had to be led to Damascus by his traveling companions. It was there that he met Ananias, a disciple of Jesus whom God would use to restore Saul's sight.

Understandably, Ananias was skeptical of this man who had been doing major harm to the saints in Jerusalem. Yet Ananias responded to the Lord's command to restore the sight of the man who would be God's instrument in taking the gospel to both the Jews and Gentiles.

My former assistant, Bonnie Purcha, remembers the time when I challenged her and a group of others to think outside the box and do something different—to be disrupted. Just like Paul, she would get a name change out of it, as well as become God's instrument for taking the gospel to the deaf community.

Bonnie told me that it was after my challenge that she began to see new ways to serve God. She asked if I would be supportive of her adopting a child as a single woman. I supported this decision that ultimately led Bonnie to making a lifelong commitment to the deaf community.

Her relationship with my niece Erica, who is hearing impaired, had inspired her to consider adopting a hearing impaired child. Bonnie enrolled in sign language classes from instructor Bill Rennie, and in a very short time I realized that Bonnie had a crush on Bill. That is how she got her name changed (in a gentler way than Paul did), and it also led to my losing her as an amazing assistant.

More than twenty-three years ago, Bonnie and Bill Rennie started the Sign Language Factory in Anaheim, California, and it has served the deaf community all over the United States. They have volunteered at Rancho Sordo Mudo, Mexico—an orphanage for the hearing impaired—and they adopted twins from a couple whose parental rights had been terminated.

> *Just like Paul, she would get a name change out of it, as well as become God's instrument for taking the gospel to the deaf community.*

Just like Paul, Bonnie's life ended up looking rather different than what she had set out to do. They both left behind what was familiar to them. God used Paul, formerly known as Saul of Tarsus; and he used Bonnie Rennie, formerly known as Bonnie Purcha, to change the world! What can he do with you?

Life-Challenging

DISRUPTION

Your life challenge this month is to identify something that you hope God never asks you to do. Then commit to finding an opportunity to serve in that way. Here are some practical suggestions for ways to do this:

- Visit children in the hospital—children who have life-threatening diseases.

- Ask a server at a restaurant or a checker at the grocery store if he or she needs prayer. Follow through by praying for this person weekly. Then go back and check to see how the person is doing.
- You and a friend or parent can take lunch to a homeless person.
- Identify a disability that someone in your life has and make it your goal to learn everything you can about it. Maybe even learn sign language!

Lord, this month I commit to serving you in a way that I have never wanted to before. Help me to follow through.

Signature _____ Date _____

NOTES

1. This information is used with permission of Sherman Pemberton.

2. YWAM Publishing, *Stepping Out: A Guide to Short Term Missions* (Seattle, WA: 1996, 2010).

3. Knowledge@Wharton, January 26, 2011, http://knowledge.wharton.upenn. edu/article.cfm?articleid=2697.

4. Information in this section was taken from Dennis N. T. Perkins, *Leading at the Edge: Leadership Lessons from the Extraordinary Saga of Shackleton's Antarctic Expedition* (New York: American Management Association, 2012), xvii.

5. J. B. Phillips, quoted by Juan Carlos Ortiz, *Call to Discipleship* (Plainfield, NJ: Logos International, 1975), xii–xiii.

6. John Ortberg, *If You Want to Walk on Water, You've Got to Get Out of the Boat* (Grand Rapids, MI: Zondervan, 2001), 24.

7. Teddy Roosevelt, http://www.theodore-roosevelt.com/trsorbonnespeech. html.

8. http://en.wikipedia.org/wiki/Taiz%C3%A9_Community.

9. Henry M. Morris, *The Defenders Bible*, marginal notes for Luke 22:44, http://christiananswers.net/q-eden/edn-t018.html.

10. Fuller Youth Institute, http://fulleryouthinstitute.org/resources/books/deep-justice-in-a-broken-world. Chap Clark and Kara Powell, *Deep Justice in a Broken World: Helping Your Kids Serve Others and Right the Wrongs Around Them* (Grand Rapids, MI: Zondervan, 2007).

11. Alvin Yoder, http://salemagapeministries.blogspot.com/2011/04/who-switched-price-tags.html.

12. "State of the World's Street Children Report," vi, http://www.streetchildren.org.uk/_uploads/publications/state_of_the_world_-_violence.pdf.

13. Steve Jobs, quoted on the Ignatius Press Blog, http://insightscoop.typepad. com/2004/2011/10/what-steve-jobs-said-about-christianity-jesus-and-faith.html.

14. "Gandhi glimpsed Christ, rejecting Christianity as a false religion," March 31, 2011, http://communities.washingtontimes. com/neighborhood/no-2-religion-yes-2-faith/2011/mar/31/ gandhi-glimpsed-christ-rejected-christianity-false.

15. Francis of Assisi, www.brainyquote.com.

16. Review of David Livermore's book *Serving with Eyes Wide Open* at http://www.masters.edu/student-life/global-outreach/missions-resources.aspx.

17. Jacqueline L. Salmon, "Churches Retool Mission Trips," *Washington Post*, July 5, 2008, http://www.washingtonpost.com/wp-dyn/content/article/2008/07/04/ AR2008070402233.html?hpid=topnews.

18. Ibid.

19. Basil, Bishop of Caesarea (329–379), http://www.stbasilvallejo.org/ parishinformation/whyisstbasilgreat.html.

20. "The Church at Laodicea in Asia Minor," http://www.padfield.com/2005/ laodicea.html.

21. Augustine, www.brainyquote.com.

22. Josiah Brooks song "He Is There," http://www.lyricsfreak.com/print. php?id=574388.

23. "Great Is Thy Faithfulness . . . & Its History," College of the Open Bible, http://www.biblicalfocus.com/Hymn_Great_Is_Thy_Faith.html.

24. Oswald Chambers, *My Utmost for His Highest* (Uhrichsville, OH: Barbour Publishing, no year given; original copyright 1935), October 12 devotional.

25. Ibid.

26. Mario Sollitto, "Can Elderly Scams Be Prevented?" http://www.agingcare. com/Articles/prevent-elderly-becoming-scam-victims-138455.htm.

27. http://www.imdb.com/title/tt0044081.

28. Mary-Lou Weisman, "The History of Retirement, from Early Man to A.A.R.P.," *New York Times*, March 21, 1999, http://www.nytimes. com/1999/03/21/jobs/the-history-of-retirement-from-early-man-to-aarp. html?pagewanted=all&src=pm.

29. http://chicagocares.wordpress.com/2011/09/26/on-your-mark-get-set-go.

30. http://www.childhelp.org/pages/about.

31. Darrell L. Guder, quoted by Christine A. Scheller in "What Does It Mean to Live a Missional Life?" April 18, 2011, http://www.thehighcalling.org/leadership/what-does-it-mean-live-missional-life.

32. This source says 1/3 c rice per day for 1 billion people: http://blog.bread.org/2011/12/my-experience-with-living-in-hunger-a-reflection.html. This source says 1/2 c: http://www.sandpointveg.org/?action=register&instance=1. This site says 800 million are "chronically hungry": http://givebread.org/Home.aspx. This says, "Every six seconds another child dies from hunger": http://www.feedthehungry.org/.

33. Michael S. Wilder, "Building and Equipping Missional Families." In the book *Trained in the Fear of God: Family Ministry in Theological, Historical, and Practical Perspective*, Randy Stinson and Timothy Paul Jones, editors (Grand Rapids, MI: Kregel, 2011), 248–249.

34. John F. Kennedy, http://er.jsc.nasa.gov/seh/ricetalk.htm.

35. Howard Major, *Lives Built on Hope: Spiritual Insights from an Unlikely Missionary* (San Diego, CA: Amor Ministries, 2010), 7.

36. Ibid., 8.

37. Walter Hochstader, quoted at http://www.freedommag.org/english/spegerm/page36.htm.

38. "Five Myths on Why Young People Leave the Church," November 16, 2011, http://www.christianpost.com/news/barna-group-releases-myths-and-realities-of-young-people-leaving-the-church-62125.

39. Information in this section was taken from http://abcnews.go.com/International/story?id=81001&page=1#.T9oxNJiE47o and http://www.nkosishaven.org and conversations with Gail Johnson. Also see Jim Wooten, *We Are All the Same: A Story of a Boy's Courage and a Mother's Love* (New York: The Penguin Press, 2004).

40. "Chet Bitterman," http://en.wikipedia.org/wiki/Chet_Bitterman.

41. Mark Batterson, *In a Pit with a Lion on a Snowy Day* (New York: Multnomah Books, 2006), 24.

42. You can learn more about Mark Ritchie's mission at www.crossbritain.co.uk.

Gayla Cooper Congdon with her husband, Scott, founded Amor Ministries in 1980 in San Diego, California, because of the need they saw in Mexican orphanages. As chief spiritual officer of Amor, Gayla oversees the staff's spiritual health and communicates Amor's mission to its constituents. She speaks at conferences and churches in the United States, Canada, and the United Kingdom. Gayla and her husband have one grown son.

- Gayla has authored several articles for *Christian Standard* and *Outcomes* magazines and was a contributing author to the book *Creative Urban Youth Ministry*.
- She is a graduate of Hope International University, Fullerton, California, and has received an honorary doctorate from Northwest Christian College, Eugene, Oregon.
- Even though she travels all over the world to speak on behalf of Amor Ministries, Gayla's favorite place to speak is around a campfire.

With more than thirty years of cross-cultural experience, Gayla can speak on a wide variety of topics to audiences of all ages. Her specialty is disrupting people's lives and challenging them to see the world through the eyes of Jesus.

For more information you may contact Gayla at: gaylac@amor.org.